Study Guide
Volume 2, Chapters 14 -26

for use with

Introduction to Accounting
An Integrated Approach

Second Edition

Penne Ainsworth
University of Wyoming

Dan Deines
Kansas State University

R. David Plumlee
University of Utah

Cathy Xanthaky Larson
Middlesex Community College

Prepared by
Debra K. Kerby
Scott R. Fouch
both of Truman State University

Boston Burr Ridge, IL Dubuque, IA Madison, WI New York San Francisco St. Louis
Bangkok Bogotá Caracas Lisbon London Madrid
Mexico City Milan New Delhi Seoul Singapore Sydney Taipei Toronto

McGraw-Hill Higher Education

A Division of The McGraw-Hill Companies

Study Guide, Volume 2, Chapters 14-26 for use with
INTRODUCTION TO ACCOUNTING: AN INTEGRATED APPROACH

Copyright © 2000, 1997 by The McGraw-Hill Companies, Inc. All rights reserved.
Printed in the United States of America.
The contents of, or parts thereof, may be reproduced for use with
INTRODUCTION TO ACCOUNTING
An Integrated Approach
Penne Ainsworth, Dan Deines, R. David Plumlee, and Cathy Xanthaky Larson
provided such reproductions bear copyright notice and may not be reproduced in
any form for any other purpose without permission of the publisher.

1 2 3 4 5 6 7 8 9 0 QPD/QPD 9 0 9 8 7 6 5 4 3 2 1 0 9

ISBN 0-07-030685-0

http://www.mhhe.com

Table of Contents

Chapter 14	The Time Value of Money: A Tool for Decision Making	1
Chapter 15	Planning for Investing Activities	23
Chapter 16	Planning Investments in Human Resources and Other Noncapitalized Assets	43
Chapter 17	Planning for Equity Financing	69
Chapter 18	Planning for Debt Financing	91
Chapter 19	Recording and Communicating Equity Financing Activities	113
Chapter 20	Recording and Communicating Long-Term Debt Financing Activities	135
Chapter 21	Recording and Communicating Operational Investment Activities	157
Chapter 22	Recording and Communicating Nonoperational Investment Activities	183
Chapter 23	Firm Performance: Profitability	207
Chapter 24	Firm Performance: Financial Position	229
Chapter 25	Firm Performance: Cash Flows	253
Chapter 26	Firm Performance: A Comprehensive Evaluation	277

Chapter 14
The Time Value of Money: A Tool for Decision Making

Chapter Overview

This chapter illustrates that business planning is based on the belief that a firm will earn a satisfactory return of and return on the investments made by the creditors and owners of the firm. Risk is considered when estimating the expected return of an investment. The chapter explains three types of risk: inflation risk, business risk, and liquidity risk. The time value of money is examined in depth. The future value and present value of a dollar is illustrated. The calculation of present and future values of annuities is also presented.

The time value of money may be an unfamiliar concept. Try relating the concept of present value to situations with which you are familiar. For example, assume that your grandparents have offered to give you $1,000 three years from now when you graduate from college or some lesser amount of cash now for meeting school expenses. Since you are very short on cash right now, you decide to take the second option. Assuming your grandparents are earning 10 percent interest on their investments, what amount of cash could you ask for today that would be equivalent to $1,000 three years from now? Also think about the various lotteries. How does a state determine the annual payments for lottery winnings? These questions require an understanding of the time value of money. By the way, your grandparents should be happy to give you $750 today.

Read and Recall Questions

> **Learning Objective:**
> L.O.1. Explain the cyclical relationship of financing, investing, and operating decisions.

On what do managers first base the firm's plans for operating activities?

The planning phase starts with operating activities and ends with financing activities. Why does the performance phase reverse this sequence?

What are the three primary uses of operating profits?

In which financial statements are the results of investing activities summarized?

In which financial statements are the results of financing activities summarized?

Learning Objective:
L.O.2. Describe the distinction between return of and return on investment and the difference between rate of return and expected rate of return.

Explain the difference between return of investment and return on investment.

Why is return on investment not adequate to differentiate among investments?

How can the amounts of initial investments distort comparisons of the dollar amount of returns on investment?

Define rate of return. How is it calculated?

Is it possible for an investment to have a negative rate of return? Explain.

What is the expected rate of return?

What are the steps to determine an investment's expected rate of return?

When is an investment's actual rate of return calculated?

Learning Objective:
L.O.3. Explain the risk-return relationship.

Define risk.

What determines how much risk a person is willing to assume?

Distinguish between risk seekers and risk avoiders. Can an individual be both a risk seeker and a risk avoider? Explain.

What does impounding mean?

What is the relative risk ratio? How is it calculated?

What is an expected return?

What does a large relative risk ratio indicate?

How are risk and return related?

What is a risk premium?

What is the risk-adjusted expected rate of return?

How does the risk-adjusted expected rate of return affect the amount an investor will pay for an investment?

Who will be more likely to demand a risk premium for assuming greater risk: a risk seeker or a risk avoider? Why?

What is the risk-free rate of return?

What is inflation risk?

What is business risk?

- What is liquidity risk?

- What is the role of perception in risk and return decisions?

Learning Objective:
L.O.4. Describe the difference between simple and compound interest and how interest relates to the time value of money.

Explain the concept of the time value of money.

- What role does the interest rate assumed have on the time value of money?

What is simple interest? How is it calculated?

What is compound interest? What does compounding mean?

How frequently can interest be compounded?

Learning Objective:
L.O.5. Demonstrate how to use the future value of the amount of $1 and the present value of $1 to solve problems that involve lump-sum cash flows at different points in time.

Define future value.

What is the future value of the amount of $1? How may this concept be used?

How does the number of compoundings affect the size of the future value?

Define present value.

What is the present value of the amount of $1? How may this concept be used?

How does the number of compoundings affect the size of the present value?

What four elements are involved in all present or future value problems?

Learning Objective:
L.O.6. Demonstrate how to use the future value of an annuity and the present value of an annuity to solve problems that involve annuity cash flows.

What is an annuity?

What is the future value of an annuity?

What three things affect the amount of money that accumulates in an annuity?

How many interest periods are associated with an ordinary annuity?

When calculating the future value of an ordinary annuity, how is the interest rate to be used determined?

What is the present value of an annuity?

Assume you are trying to determine the future value of investing $500 every three months at an annual interest rate of 12 percent for the next four years. What is the interest rate and number of periods to be used in determining the future value of the annuity?

What are the four steps for solving an annuity problem?

What are two business applications of the time value of money?

Outline of Key Concepts

I. The management cycle includes operating, investing, and financing decisions.
    A. Operating decisions involve using the organization's resources to generate an operating profit.
    B. Investing decisions involve determining how to invest the funds obtained.
        1. Funds are invested in either current assets or long-term assets.
    C. Financing decisions involve determining the amount of funds needed and the sources of obtaining the funds.
        1. Funds may be acquired through debt financing or equity financing.

II. There is a difference between return of and return on investment.
    A. Return of investment is the return of the initial investment to the owner.
    B. Return on investment is the money received in excess of the initial investment.

C. Rate of return measures the performance of investments on a common-size basis and eliminates any distortion caused by the size of the initial investment.
   1. The rate is usually expressed as an annual rate.
   2. The rate of return on investment does not consider the length of time that investments are held.
D. The expected rate of return is the predicted return rate based on the possible rates of return and the likelihood of those rates of return occurring.
   1. Investors estimate the expected rate of return before making the investment.

III. Risk is the exposure to the chance than an unfavorable outcome will occur at some future point in time.
   A. Attitudes toward risk determine the amount of risk that people are willing to assume.
      1. Risk seekers are people who enjoy risky situations.
      2. Risk avoiders are those who avoid risk.
      3. The decision under consideration may affect the decision-maker's normal attitude toward risk.
   B. The risk of any investment is impounded in the expected rate of return.
      1. The relative risk ratio reflects the risk of an investment as a percentage of the expected return lost if the worst-case outcome occurs.
         a. The amount of risk depends on the difference between the worst possible outcome and the expected rate of return.
         b. The larger the relative risk ratio, the higher an investment's risk.
   C. Risk and return are directly related, that is, the greater the risk, the greater the return the investor expects.
      1. Investors select investments with the highest expected return for a given level of risk.
      2. Risk premium--the increase in the expected rate of return that compensates the investor for assuming increased risk.
      3. Risk-adjusted expected rate of return--an expected rate of return including the risk premium.
         a. When the risk-adjusted expected rate of return increases, an investor pays less for the investment.
   D. Risk factors determine the expected return.
      1. Risk-free rate of return--return that a virtually riskless investment produces.
      2. Inflation risk--chance of decline in purchasing power of the monetary units during the time the money is invested.
      3. Business risk--reflects the likelihood of a company ceasing normal operations.
      4. Liquidity risk--chance that an investment cannot be readily converted into cash.

IV. Time value of money is the concept that implies that a dollar today, given that it can generate a return on investment over time, is worth more than a dollar one year from today.
   A. Simple interest--calculated only on the amount borrowed.
      1. Interest = Principal x Interest rate x Time

B. Compound interest--interest that is based on a principal amount that includes interest from previous time periods.
C. Future value of the amount of $1--amount that $1 becomes at a future date, if invested at a specified annual interest rate and compounded a certain number of times per year over the investment period.
   1. It is a means of determining the amount of money in the future that is equivalent to an amount today.
   2. The future value increases as the frequency of compounding increases.
D. Present value of the amount of $1--cash equivalent today of some specified amount of cash at a specified date in the future.
   1. It is equivalent to the future amount less the interest that has accumulated over the intervening time period.
   2. It is the reciprocal of the future value of the amount of $1.
   3. The present value decreases as the number of compounding periods increases.
E. All present or future value problems involve four elements.
   1. The interest rate for each compounding period.
   2. The number of compounding periods.
   3. The present value amount
   4. The future value amount.
F. Future value of an annuity--amount of money that accumulates at some future date as a result of making equal payments over equal intervals of time and earning a specified interest rate over that time period.
   1. Use the future value of annuities to determine the amount to save on a regular basis to buy new assets or retire debt at some future date.
   2. Ordinary annuity--assumes that the final payment is made on the future value date, so there is one less interest period than the number of payments.
G. Present value of an annuity--amount of money that, if invested at some interest rate today, will generate a set number of periodic payments that are made over equal time intervals.
H. Solving annuity problems uses a four-step process.
   1. Determine whether the problem is an annuity.
   2. Determine whether the annuity is a present value or future value.
      a. With the future value of an annuity, the lump sum or future value occurs after the annuity payments are made.
      b. In the case of the present value annuity, the lump sum or present value precedes the annuity payments.
   3. Identify the missing annuity element.
   4. Solve for the missing element.
I. Time value of money is used in business applications.
   1. Determine asset valuation.
   2. Financial planning for college education or retirement.

©The McGraw-Hill Companies, Inc., 2000

Problem I

Indicate whether the following statements are either true (T) or false (F).

_____ 1. An investment will have a negative rate of return if the original investment is not recovered.
_____ 2. The predicted rate of return on an investment is called the annual rate of return.
_____ 3. People who enjoy taking risks are said to be risk avoiders.
_____ 4. There is a direct relationship between the uncertainty that an unfavorable outcome will occur and the level of risk of an investment.
_____ 5. The amount/cost of an investment varies inversely with the change in its risk-adjusted rate of return.
_____ 6. Inflation risk is factored into every investment decision.
_____ 7. To earn a higher rate of return, the investor must assume more risk.
_____ 8. The higher the probability of default on a loan, the lower the interest rate charged on the debt.
_____ 9. The present value of future cash flows will always be smaller than the sum of those future cash flows.
_____ 10. Business risk takes into account the likelihood that a company will cease operations.

Problem II

Indicate the correct answer by circling the appropriate letter.

1. Investment Z cost $5,000 and was sold one year later for $5,900. The investment's rate of return was
   a. 8%
   b. 12%
   c. 14%
   d. 18%

2. Which of the following risk factors will result in a risk premium being included in the risk-adjusted rate of return on an investment?
   a. inflation risk
   b. business risk
   c. liquidity risk
   d. all of the above

3. Max, age 25, wants to retire a millionaire in 20 years. If Max's investments average a 12% rate of return (compounded annually), how much must he invest at the end of each year in order to have $1,000,000 at retirement?
   a. $13,879
   b. $12,679
   c. $15,638
   d. $22,465

4. Mary wants to purchase a new automobile in five years that will cost $30,000. Assuming that she can earn a 6% annual rate of return, how much must she invest today to insure she will have the $30,000?
   a. $25,674
   b. $21,111
   c. $16,784
   d. $22,419

5. How would your answer change to question (4) if Mary earned 6% compounded semi-annually?
   a. $24,187
   b. $22,345
   c. $22,323
   d. $21,785

6. Yolanda recently inherited $300,000. She intends to invest $100,000 of the inheritance and spend the rest. If her investment earns 4% compounded semi-annually, how much will she have in 15 years?
   a. $181,140
   b. $165,450
   c. $185,680
   d. $220,650

7. Determine the present value of a $10,000 annuity payments made over ten years if the payments are made at the end of each year. The annuity earns an 8% annual rate of return.
   a. $67,101
   b. $63,456
   c. $56,091
   d. $83,423

8. Jean purchased a $25,000 automobile and must make annual payments of $6,595 for the next five years. What annual rate of interest is Jean being charged on the loan?
   a. 6%
   b. 8%
   c. 10%
   d. 12%

©The McGraw-Hill Companies, Inc., 2000

9. John plans to invest $20,000 in a certificate of deposit that will earn 5% annually. Approximately how many years will it take to double his investment?
   a. 5
   b. 10
   c. 15
   d. 20

10. Bill and Mary need to borrow $200,000 to purchase a house in the country. If the annual interest rate is 12% and the repayment period is 15 years, their yearly loan payment will be _____.
    a. $21,894
    b. $31,510
    c. $29,365
    d. $34,321

Problem III

Following is a list of important ideas and key concepts from the chapter. To test your knowledge of these terms, match the term with the definition by placing the number in the space provided.

_____ annuity
_____ business risk
_____ compounding
_____ expected return
_____ future value
_____ future value of an annuity
_____ inflation risk
_____ liquidity risk
_____ present value
_____ present value of an annuity
_____ rate of return
_____ relative risk ratio
_____ risk-adjusted expected rate of return
_____ risk-free rate of return
_____ risk premium
_____ time value of money

1. A common-size measure of an investment's risk based on the percentage of expected return lost if the worst-case outcome occurs

2. A series of equal cash payments made at equal intervals

3. The amount of money that accumulates at some future date as a result of making equal payments over equal intervals of time and earning a specified rate of interest over that time period

4. A tool used to solve problems involving the comparison of cash flows that occur at different points in time

5. The process of adding interest to principal for purposes of interest calculation

6. The chance that an investment cannot be readily converted to cash

7. An expected rate of return including the risk premium

8. The chance of a decline in the purchasing power of the monetary units during the time money is invested

9. A summary measure of an investment's performance stated in dollars that is based on the dollar amount of the possible returns on investment and the probability of those returns occurring

10. The rate of return that a virtually riskless investment produces

11. The amount of money that, if invested at some rate of interest today, will generate a set number of equal periodic payments that are made over equal time intervals

12. The risk associated with the ability of a particular company to continue in business

13. The combination of principal and the interest on the principal at some specified date in the future

14. The cash equivalent today of some specified amount of cash at a specified date in the future

15. A percentage measurement of the performance of investments on a common-size basis

16. An increase in the rate of return expected by an investor for assuming greater investment risk

Problem IV

Complete the following sentences by filling in the correct response.

1. Return on investment should not be used to rank investment alternatives because it does not take into account the _____ the investment was held or the _____ of the initial investment.

2. The expected rate of return is based on the _____ rates of return and the _____ of those rates of return occurring.

3. Because the relative risk ratio is a _____ measure, it is possible to rank respective risks of different investment alternatives from high to low.

4. The _____ the relative risk ratio, the greater the risk of the investment.

5. The time value of money is the tool used to solve problems involving cash flows that occur at _____ points in time.

6. The cash equivalent today of some specified amount of cash at a specified date in the future is called the _____ _____ of that future amount.

7. An annuity is a series of _____ cash payments over equal time periods.

8. Investors will choose the investment with the _____ expected return for a given level of _____.

Problem V

Calculate the expected rate of return on a $200,000 investment with following possible outcomes (returns will occur at the end of one year):

Possible Outcomes	Possible Returns	Probability of Outcome
Robust economy	$ 90,000	.15
Steady growth	20,000	.65
Recession	4,000	.15
Depression	$-70,000	.05

Problem VI

The following information is provided for two investment alternatives:

	Investment X	Investment Y
Amount of investment	$50,000	$50,000
Possible outcomes and (probabilities)	10,000 (.8)	15,000 (.7)
	4,000 (.2)	1,000 (.3)

a. Calculate the expected rate or return for each investment.

b. Calculate the relative risk ratio for each investment.

Pause and Reflect

Furniture stores frequently offer sales with terms of no money down and no payments or interest for one year. How do furniture stores recover the interest lost by such financing arrangements?

Solutions for Chapter 14

Problem I

1. T
2. F
3. F
4. T
5. T

6. T
7. T
8. F
9. T
10. T

Problem II

1. d
2. d
3. a
4. d
5. c
6. a
7. a
8. c
9. c
10. c

Problem III

- 2 annuity
- 12 business risk
- 5 compounding
- 9 expected return
- 13 future value
- 3 future value of an annuity
- 8 inflation risk
- 6 liquidity risk
- 14 present value
- 11 present value of an annuity
- 15 rate of return
- 1 relative risk ratio
- 7 risk-adjusted expected rate of return
- 10 risk-free rate of return
- 16 risk premium
- 4 time value of money

Problem IV

1. time, amount
2. possible, likelihood
3. common-size
4. larger
5. different
6. present value
7. equal
8. highest, risk

Problem V

Possible Outcomes	Possible Returns	Rate of Return if Event Occurs	Probability of Outcome
Robust economy	$ 90,000	45%	.15
Steady growth	20,000	10%	.65
Recession	4,000	2%	.15
Depression	$-70,000	-35%	.05

Expected rate of return = (.15 x 45%) + (.65 x 10%) + (.15 x 2%) + (.05 x -35%) = 11.8%

Problem VI

a. Investment X   Expected rate of return = (.8 x 20%) + (.2 x 8%) = 17.6%

    Investment Y   Expected rate of return = (.7 x 30%) + (.3 x 2%) = 21.6%

b. Investment X   Relative risk ratio = $\dfrac{17.6\% - 8\%}{17.6\%}$ = 54.5%

    Investment Y   Relative risk ratio = $\dfrac{21.6\% - 2\%}{21.6\%}$ = 90.7%

Pause and Reflect

The furniture stores use the market rate of interest to determine the opportunity cost of postponing cash collections for the sale. This opportunity cost is taken into consideration when the sales price of the furniture is determined.

Chapter 15
Planning for Investing Activities

Chapter Overview

Chapter 15 applies the time value of money concepts of Chapter 14 to capital budgeting. Capital budgeting is a process used to decide which investments to acquire and to evaluate the performance of the investments after acquisition. The chapter identifies the steps of the capital budgeting process and describes discounted cash flow analysis. The net present value method of analysis is emphasized, but the time-adjusted rate of return is also presented. Income tax and depreciation effects on the capital budgeting process are explored.

Success in learning Chapter 15 materials requires a good understanding of the time value of money concepts presented in Chapter 14. If you do not understand the time value of money, you should review Chapter 14 problems before proceeding with this chapter. When completing net present value problems, first focus on identifying the cash inflows and cash outflows as lump sum amounts or annuities. Make sure you use the appropriate interest rates and interest compounding periods. Remember that depreciation is not a cash flow, but because depreciation is a tax-deductible expense it reduces income tax payments and thus has cash flow consequences. Although you may be inclined to think that the capital budgeting results tell a manager what investment decision to make, any investment decision must be tempered by sound judgments about the underlying assumptions made about cash flows, interest rates, and time.

Read and Recall Questions

> **Learning Objective:**
> L.O.1. Describe the capital budgeting process.

What is capital budgeting?

Who should be involved in the capital budgeting process?

What are the four basic processes in capital budgeting?

What types of expenditures are included in the cost of a firm's long-term operational investments?

What are the three significant reasons why companies make capital investments?

Why are strategic planning documents important to identify capital investment opportunities?

What is the cost of capital?

- What does it mean when an investment's return is greater than the cost of capital?

- Why is the cost of capital sometimes referred to as the hurdle rate?

- What two choices does a firm have for financing its capital expenditures?

- What information is presented in the capital expenditure budget? In the financing budget?

- What type of evaluation of capital expenditures occurs in the acquisition phase?

What type of evaluation of capital expenditures occurs in the postaudit?

What role do accountants play in capital budgeting?

What is discounted cash flow analysis?

Learning Objective:
L.O.2. Explain and apply the net present value method of discounted cash flow analysis.

Explain the net present value (NPV) method of discounted cash flow analysis.

Using the net present value method, when is an investment acceptable?

What are the four steps involved in the net present value method?

What does a positive net present value mean?

Does net present value represent the amount of profit or loss that the asset will realize? Explain.

Can NPV be used if cash flows are uneven? Explain.

Learning Objective:
L.O.3. Describe the time-adjusted rate of return method of discounted cash flow analysis.

What is the time-adjusted rate of return (TARR)? What is another common name for the TARR?

What are the three steps in applying the TARR?

What does it mean if the TARR is less than the hurdle rate (cost of capital)?

What are the advantages and disadvantages associated with the TARR?

What major advantage does NPV have over the TARR?

What are the three assumptions underlying discounted cash flow analysis?

What are some examples of typical cash outflows associated with capital investments? Examples of typical cash inflows?

Learning Objective:
L.O.4. Explain the impact of taxes on the net present value method.

How do income taxes affect capital budgeting decisions?

Define after-tax cash flows.

What are after-tax cash inflows? What is the formula for determining after-tax cash inflows?

What are after-tax cash outflows? What is the formula for determining after-tax cash outflows?

If depreciation is a noncash expense, how can it have an effect on investment decisions when discounted cash flow analysis is being used to guide management decisions?

What are the two sources of cash flows associated with the disposal of old assets?

How are the net-of-tax cash flows from an asset sold with a gain calculated?

How are the net-of-tax cash flows from an asset sold with a loss determined?

Learning Objective:
L.O.5. Describe how judgment and uncertainty impact the capital budgeting process.

What difference in assumptions exists between discounted cash flow analysis and accrual accounting?

What is meant by the term "informed speculation"?

What is sensitivity analysis? Why may sensitivity analysis be used when making capital investment decisions?

What qualitative factors should be considered when making capital investment decisions?

Outline of Key Concepts

I. Capital budgeting is a process that managers use for analysis and selection of the long-term investments of a business. Capital budgeting consists of four basic processes.
   A. Identifying long-term investment opportunities.
      1. Must determine what expenditures are included in the cost of long-term investments.
      2. Must identify the reasons that companies make capital investments.
         a. To replace worn out or unproductive operating assets.
         b. To expand the business's operating capacity.
         c. To comply with government mandates.
   B. Selecting appropriate investments.
      1. Cost of capital--weighted-average cost of a firm's debt and equity financing.
         a. It represents the amount of return that the assets of the firm must generate in order to satisfy both creditors and owners.
         b. When the rate of return on assets meets or exceeds the cost of capital, both creditors and stockholders are satisfied.

C. Financing the selected investments.
   1. A firm has a choice of using debt or equity financing.
D. Evaluating investments.
   1. Acquisition phase--monitor costs incurred in conjunction with the asset's acquisition.
   2. Postaudit--compare the cash flow projections made in the preacquisition analysis with the actual cash flows generated by the asset.

II. Discounted cash flow analysis is a method to evaluate investments that uses the time value of money to assess whether the investment's expected rate of return is greater than the firm's cost of capital.
   A. Net present value (NPV)--requires that decision-makers find the present value of an investment's estimated future cash flows by using the firm's cost of capital as a discount rate. The NPV method consists of the following four steps.
      1. Identify the timing and amount of all cash inflows and outflows associated with the potential investment.
      2. Calculate the present value of the future cash flows using the firm's cost of capital as the discount rate.
      3. Compute the net present value by subtracting the initial cash outflows necessary to acquire the asset from the present value of the future cash inflows.
      4. Decide to accept or reject the investment in the capital asset.
         a. If the net present value is zero or positive, the proposed investment is acceptable.
         b. If the net present value is negative, the company should reject the project.
         c. Present value of the future cash flows represents the maximum price that should be paid for the investment.
         d. NPV does not represent the amount of profit or loss that the asset will realize.
   B. Time-adjusted rate of return (TARR) equals the rate of return on the investment given the future cash flows.
      1. The TARR is compared to the cost of capital to see if it is higher or lower than the hurdle rate.
      2. The TARR method has three steps.
         a. Identify the timing and amount of all cash inflows and outflows associated with the investment.
         b. Determine the time-adjusted rate of return.
         c. Decide to accept or reject the investment. Accept the investment if its TARR is greater than or equal to the cost of capital, otherwise, reject the investment.
   C. Advantages and disadvantages of discounted cash flow methods.
      1. TARR.
         a. Advantage--once TARR is calculated, the decision about whether to make the investment is straightforward.
         b. Disadvantage--time-consuming, trial-and-error process is required when dealing with uneven cash flows.

c. Disadvantage--cannot be adjusted for risk.
2. NPV.
   a. Advantage--easier to compute than TARR.
   b. Advantage--can be adjusted for risk.
D. There are three key assumptions underlying discounted cash flow analysis.
   1. All cash flows are known with certainty.
   2. Cash flows are assumed to occur at the end of each time period.
   3. Cash inflows are immediately reinvested in another project that earns a return for the company.
E. Sources of cash flows.
   1. Cash outflows include the initial acquisition cost, other acquisition-related costs such as freight, sales tax, and installation charges, and required increases in working capital.
   2. Cash inflows include revenues and decreased operating expenses.
F. After-tax cost flows are the estimated cash flows associated with a potential investment after considering the impact of income taxes.
   1. After-tax cash inflow is the difference between the taxable cash inflow and the amount of tax paid on it.
      a. After-tax cash inflow = Taxable cash inflows x (1 - Tax rate)
   2. After-tax cash outflows are smaller than pretax cash payments because pretax cash payments reduce the income subject to tax, and therefore, reduce the firm's income taxes.
      a. After-tax cash outflow = Deductible cash outflow x (1 - Tax rate)
   3. Noncash expenses, like depreciation, do not directly decrease cash.
      a. They reduce income subject to tax and the related amount of income taxes.
      b. Tax shields reduce the potential amount of a firm's tax liability by reducing its taxable income.
      c. They keep firms from being taxed on the recovery of the cost of their investments.
   4. Gains and losses on disposal of investments.
      a. Gain on disposal--occurs if the proceeds from the sale of an asset exceed its book value at the date of disposal. Taxes reduce the proceeds of the sale.
         Net-of-tax cash flows from an asset sold with a gain =
            Proceeds from disposal - (Gain on disposal x Tax rate)
      b. Loss on disposal--occurs if the proceeds from the sale of an asset are less than its book value at the date of the sale. Tax effects increase the net cash proceeds from disposal.
         Net-of-tax cash flows from an asset sold with a loss =
            Proceeds from disposal + (Loss on disposal x Tax rate)
G. Discounted cash flows and accrual accounting are based on different assumptions.
   1. Discounted cash flow considers only the amount and timing of cash flows.
   2. Accrual accounting measures the economic consequences of business transactions, whether or not cash was a part of the transaction.

©The McGraw-Hill Companies, Inc., 2000

H. Capital budgeting decisions require the personal judgment of decision-makers.
   1. Personal perceptions can affect the forecasting of future cash flows resulting in uncertainty in the capital budgeting process.
   2. Sensitivity analysis is used to evaluate how a change in estimated cash flows or discount rates might affect the capital budgeting decision.
   3. Managers must also consider certain qualitative factors in their decisions.

Problem I

Indicate whether the following statements are either true (T) or false (F).

_____ 1. If the time-adjusted rate of return is greater than the cost of capital, the investment is acceptable.

_____ 2. To be acceptable, an investment's rate of return must exceed the company's cost of capital.

_____ 3. The net present value of an investment is the profit generated by the investment.

_____ 4. The rate of return used to determine present value is called the discount rate.

_____ 5. A decrease in operating expenses would be considered a cash inflow.

_____ 6. Discounted cash flow analysis does not take into account the time value of money.

_____ 7. If the net present value of a project is negative, the investment should not be undertaken.

_____ 8. An advantage of the time-adjusted rate of return method is that it can be adjusted for different levels of risk.

_____ 9. After-tax cash outflows are smaller than the pretax cash payment.

_____ 10. A depreciation tax shield will be treated as a cash inflow.

Problem II

Indicate the correct answer by circling the appropriate letter.

1. Which of the following is not a basic process involved in capital budgeting?
   a. Identifying long-term investment opportunities.
   b. Selecting the appropriate investments.
   c. Financing the selected investments.
   d. Evaluating the investments.
   e. All of the above are basic processes in capital budgeting.

2. Which of the following is not a reason for a company to make a long-term investment?
   a. To replace worn out or unproductive equipment.
   b. To avoid paying dividends on stock.
   c. To expand the business's operating capacity.
   d. To comply with mandates of the government.
   e. All of the above are reasons for making long-term investments.

3. Corporation X is financed by using $3,000,000 of stockholders' equity and $2,000,000 of debt. If the debt has an 8 percent interest rate and stockholders require a 15 percent return on their investment, the cost of capital will be _____.
   a. 12.2 percent
   b. 11.7 percent
   c. 11.5 percent
   d. 23 percent

4. Which of the following is not an assumption underlying discounted cash flow analysis?
   a. All cash flows are known with certainty.
   b. Cash flows occur at the beginning of the period.
   c. Cash flows are immediately invested in another project that earns a return meeting or exceeding the cost of capital.
   d. All of the above are assumptions of discounted cash flow analysis.

5. Company Z sold a machine for $50,000. The machine had a book value of $70,000 and the company's effective income tax rate was 40 percent. The after-tax cash inflow from the sale was _____.
   a. $46,000
   b. $50,000
   c. $58,000
   d. $70,000

6. Company Y is considering an investment that will cost $1,977,570 and will generate annual cash inflows of $350,000 for the next ten years. Ignoring the effect of taxes, the investment's time-adjusted rate of return is _____.
   a. 8 percent
   b. 10 percent
   c. 12 percent
   d. 14 percent

7. Company Z can acquire a machine that will reduce annual operating costs by $20,000 for the next five years. Assuming a cost of capital of 16 percent and ignoring the effect of taxes, what is the maximum price the company would be willing to pay for the machine?
   a. $65,486
   b. $61,785
   c. $83,456
   d. $100,000

8. Company X sold a machine for $100,000. The machine had a book value of $90,000 and the company's effective income tax rate was 30 percent. The after-tax cash inflow from the sale was _____.
   a. $90,000
   b. $93,000
   c. $97,000
   d. $100,000

9. Alpha Corporation is considering a $200,000 investment that will produce annual cash inflows of $30,000 for the next 15 years. Alpha's cost of capital is 12 percent. Ignoring the effect of taxes, the investment's net present value will be _____.
   a. <$25,650>
   b. $1,456
   c. $14,897
   d. $4,327

10. Zeta Company is considering investing in a project that will generate the following cash inflows:

Year	Cash Inflow
1	$35,000
2	$45,000
3	$60,000

Ignoring taxes and assuming a 10 percent cost of capital, what is the maximum price the company would pay for the project?
   a. $114,085
   b. $116,782
   c. $139,789
   d. $140,000

11. Company Y has invested in equipment that will generate annual pre-tax operating expense savings of $100,000. Depreciation on the equipment is $20,000 per year. Assuming an effective tax rate of 30 percent, the <u>net</u> annual cash flow from the equipment is _____.
   a. $120,000
   b. $84,000
   c. $76,000
   d. $36,000

Problem III

Following is a list of important ideas and key concepts from the chapter. To test your knowledge of these terms, match the term with the definition by placing the number in the space provided.

_____ capital budgeting
_____ capital expenditure budget
_____ cost of capital
_____ discounted cash flow analysis

_____ financing budget
_____ net present value
_____ tax shield
_____ time-adjusted rate of return

1. A method to evaluate investments that uses the time value of money to assess whether the investment's expected rate of return is greater than a firm's cost of capital

2. A noncash expense that reduces the potential amount of a firm's tax liability by reducing its taxable income without affecting its pretax cash flows

3. A budget that outlines the amounts and sources of funds needed to finance the firm's investments for the designated time period

4. The process used for analysis and selection of the long-term investments of a business

5. A discounted cash flow method that requires using the cost of a potential investment as the present value of the projected cash flows in order to determine the rate of return on the proposed investment

6. A discounted cash flow analysis that requires decision makers find the present value of an investment's estimated future cash flows by using the firm's cost of capital as the discount rate

7. A weighted-average cost of a firm's debt and equity financing

8. A budget that describes the amount and timing of the capital expenditures planned for the designated time period

Problem IV

Zectar Corporation is considering investing $500,000 in a machine that will produce annual operating income of $200,000 for five years. Depreciation on the machine would be $60,000 per year. The company's effective tax rate is 30 percent and its discount rate is 16 percent.

   a. Calculate the after-tax cash flows associated with the project.

   b. Calculate the net present value of the investment.

   c. Should the investment be undertaken? Why?

Problem V

Complete the following sentences by filling in the correct response.

1. A firm's cost of capital is the weighted average cost of a firm's _____ and _____ financing.

2. The _____ phase of evaluation involves the comparison of the cash flow projections made in the preacquisition analysis to the _____ cash flows generated by the investment.

3. Under the _____ _____ _____ method, the cost of capital is used as the discount rate.

4. The _____ _____ _____ is the return that is necessary to satisfy both creditors and owners.

5. Discounted cash flow methods only consider the _____ and _____ of an investment's cash flows.

Pause and Reflect

Investment opportunities with a negative net present value (NPV) are not usually considered to be acceptable opportunities. Under what circumstances should an investment project with a negative NPV be considered a viable alternative?

_____
_____
_____
_____
_____
_____
_____
_____
_____
_____
_____
_____
_____
_____
_____
_____

Solutions for Chapter 15

Problem I

1. T
2. T
3. F
4. T
5. T
6. F
7. T
8. F
9. T
10. T

Problem II

1. e
2. b
3. a
4. b
5. c
6. c
7. a
8. c
9. d
10. a
11. c

Problem III

4	capital budgeting	3	financing budget
8	capital expenditure budget	6	net present value
7	cost of capital	2	tax shield
1	discounted cash flow analysis	5	time-adjusted rate of return

Problem IV

a. **After-tax Cash Flows**
   Cost of machine   <$500,000>
   Annual operating income   (1 - .30) x $200,000 = $140,000
   Annual depreciation   (.30) x $ 60,000 = $ 18,000

b. **Net Present Value**
   Pva (5, 16%) x $140,000   3.2744 x $140,000 = $458,416
   Pva (5, 16%) x $ 18,000   3.2744 x $ 18,000 = $ 58,939
       Net cash inflows $517,355
       Less: Cost of machine   <$500,000>
       Net Present Value $ 17,355

c. Since the net present value is positive, the company should make the investment. The return on the investment exceeds the cost of the company's capital.

Problem V

1. debt, equity
2. postaudit, actual
3. net present value
4. cost of capital
5. amount, timing

Pause and Reflect

If the investment opportunity is showing a small negative NPV, the project may still be considered. The decision maker would evaluate the reasonableness of the interest rate used to discount the cash flows. The decision maker would consider whether the rate accurately reflects the riskiness of the project. If the decision maker believes the discount rate overstates the riskiness of the project, the project may be considered acceptable. In addition, the accuracy of the amount and timing of cash flow estimates may be questioned. As a result, sensitivity analysis may be undertaken. Differing rates of interest may be used to assess the sensitivity of the results to changes in interest rates, or differing cash flow estimates may be used to test the model.

Qualitative factors may also be considered. Even with a negative NPV, a project may be considered desirable if it enhances quality or customer service. The project may also assist a company in meeting social or legal responsibilities.

Chapter 16
Planning Investments in Human Resources and Other Noncapitalized Assets

Chapter Overview

In the last chapter, investments in long-term capital assets were discussed. This chapter explores the equally important investment in human resources. Management strives to attain effective and efficient use of the firm's human resources. To accomplish this, managers must understand the costs and benefits of employee recruitment, selection, training, development, and retention. Chapter 16 also examines employee compensation and benefits. The chapter concludes by presenting the balanced scorecard as an approach for motivating and evaluating the outcomes of employees' activities.

As you read this chapter, you may wonder why issues like employee recruitment, employee evaluation, and motivation theories are included in an accounting textbook. The text has emphasized that accounting information has decision usefulness in a variety of business contexts. Accounting information systems can be used to collect the costs and benefits of employee recruitment, selection, training, and retention. Clearly payroll and compensation issues are linked into accounting systems. Accountants also collect financial and nonfinancial information that can be used to motivate and evaluate employee actions. Think about your own work experiences, and draw connections between the human resource function and the accounting function.

Read and Recall Questions

Learning Objective:
L.O.1. Explain what a company's human resources are and how they are linked to its strategy.

What are noncapitalized assets? Why is human capital considered a noncapitalized asset?

What is human resources (HR) management?

Distinguish between a mechanistic organizational structure and an organic organizational structure.

Define organizational strategy.

Distinguish between an efficiency strategy and a flexibility strategy.

Learning Objective:
L.O.2. Describe the costs incurred in and the benefits derived from employee recruitment, selection, training, and development processes.

What are the four steps of human resources planning?

What types of questions must be answered to determine job skills needed in the future?

What types of questions should be asked to assess the skills of the current workforce?

What types of questions should be asked to assess the future supply of human capital?

What items should be included in a strategic plan for obtaining human capital?

Identify at least four recruitment and selection costs associated with a human resources department.

What are the benefits of a recruitment and selection strategy?

What items might be included in an employee orientation program?

What are the benefits of employee training programs?

Learning Objective:
L.O.3. Describe the type and cost of benefits provided to employees during and after employment.

Distinguish among the following pay plans: piece-rate pay, commission pay, hourly pay, and salary pay.

Why do companies pay for health and life insurance for their employees?

Why do companies offer employees paid or unpaid leaves?

What is a bonus? Why are bonuses offered to employees?

Define bonus rate and bonus base.

What is deferred compensation?

How might an employee benefit from receiving deferred cash compensation?

What is a stock option plan? What are the benefits to a company of a stock option plan?

What are the benefits of a stock option plan to an employee?

Identify three post-retirement benefits that may be available to employees.

Distinguish between a defined contribution plan and a defined benefit plan for post-retirement benefits.

What does it mean when a benefit plan is vested?

What is the difference between a contributory plan and noncontributory plan?

What is the difference between a funded plan and unfunded plan?

Learning Objective:
L.O.4. Explain how a company uses the balanced scorecard approach to manage its other noncapitalized assets.

What benefits do companies receive from noncapitalized assets?

What is the balanced scorecard? What four perspectives are included in a typical balanced scorecard?

What types of measures are included in the financial perspective of the balanced scorecard?

Where are measures relating to quality, supplier relationships, and innovation reported in the balanced scorecard? How do these measures help a company achieve its strategic objectives?

Identify at least three measures related to customer acquisition, satisfaction, and retention.

How are the internal process and customer perspectives related?

How do companies monitor the learning and growth perspective of the balanced scorecard?

How are the internal process perspective and learning and growth perspective related?

What is goal incongruence? How does the balanced scorecard overcome goal incongruence?

Appendix:

Learning Objective:
L.O.5. Compare and contrast motivation and leadership theories and their implications for employee evaluation and reward systems.

Describe Maslow's hierarchy of needs. How does Maslow's theory relate to employee compensation and rewards?

Herzberg's theory focuses on two sets of needs--hygiene factors and motivator factors. How do these factors differ?

What are the implications of Herzberg's theory of motivation for employee evaluation and reward?

Describe Vroom's expectancy theory of motivation.

©The McGraw-Hill Companies, Inc., 2000

McGregor believed that managers have two different attitudes about employees that lead to different leadership styles, Theory X attitude and Theory Y attitude. Distinguish between Theory X and Theory Y attitudes.

Identify and define four types of power.

What are the implications of leadership and power theories on compensation and reward systems?

Outline of Key Concepts

I. Human capital is an important noncapitalized asset.
    A. Noncapitalized assets--items that have future value but do not qualify as assets.
    B. Human resources management--policies and procedures companies use to ensure effective and efficient use of their human capital.
       1. A company's external environment impacts human resources management.
          a. Mechanistic organizational structure--activities and employees are arranged by functions, control is maintained at the top of the hierarchy, and rules and regulations are followed.
          b. Organic organizational structure--activities and people are arranged by cross-functional teams, decision making is decentralized, and there are few formalized rules and regulations.
       2. Organizational strategy--a company's long-term plan for using its resources including its human capital.

        a. Efficiency strategy--focuses on reducing costs or containing costs, improving productivity, and penetrating the market with products and services by having the lowest cost.
        b. Flexibility strategy--strives to adapt to changing market conditions by expanding (or contracting) product lines, customer bases, and markets.

II.   Human resources management requires planning.
    A. Human resources planning consists of four steps.
       1. Determine job skills needed in the future.
       2. Assess the skills of the current workforce.
       3. Determine the future supply of human capital.
       4. Prepare a strategic plan for obtaining human capital.
    B. Recruitment and selection of employees result in costs and benefits.
       1. Costs include the following:
          a. Salaries paid to HR employees.
          b. Costs of advertising for positions.
          c. Costs incurred for recordkeeping.
          d. Costs incurred to conduct employment tests and/or background investigations of potential employees.
       2. Benefits of a good recruitment and selection process include the following:
          a. Minimizes the chance of hiring incompetent or unproductive employees.
          b. Ensures a good fit between the company and the employee.
          c. Indicates compliance with labor laws.
    C. Training and development of employees result in costs and benefits.
       1. Costs include the following:
          a. Costs of orientation activities.
          b. Costs of formal or informal training activities.
          c. Costs of employee mistakes while learning the job.
       2. Benefits of a good training and development process include the following:
          a. Employees are less likely to make costly mistakes.
          b. Employees are more likely to continue their employment with the company.
          c. Employees may be trained to do more than one job and are more adaptable.

III.   Employees received numerous benefits from their employers.
    A. Companies use a variety of pay plans.
       1. Piece-rate pay--compensation is based on the number of items completed.
       2. Commission pay--a percentage of revenue generated.
       3. Hourly pay--a certain amount per hour with perhaps more per hour for overtime.
       4. Salary pay--a fixed amount per period, typically one month.
    B. Firms offer many forms of fringe benefits.
       1. Health and life insurance.
       2. Paid leave such as sick days, family leave, and vacation time.
       3. Bonuses--compensation that is contingent on the occurrence of some future event.

  a. May be based on income before bonus or income taxes, on income before taxes, or net income.
 C. Deferred compensation--employee benefit that is earned in one period and paid out in a future period.
  1. Deferred cash compensation--employee may benefit if a lower tax rate is expected in the future.
  2. Stock option plans--offer the employees the option of purchasing the company's capital stock at some specified price within some specified period of time.
 D. Post-retirement benefits--include all the benefits employees received after retirement.
  1. Pensions are a significant post-retirement benefit.
   a. Defined contribution plan--employer promises to make specific contributions to the plan, but the post-retirement benefits received by the retiree are not specified.
   b. Defined benefit plan--employer promises to pay the employee a specified amount at retirement.
  2. There are three other characteristics of benefit plans.
   a. Does the employee have the right to the benefits if employment ceases?
    i. Vested plan--has the rights to the benefit plan even if the employee is not employed at the time.
   b. Does the employee contribute personal funds to the plan?
    i. Contributory plan--an employee and his or her employee contribute to the plan.
    ii. Noncontributory plan--only the employer contributes to the plan.
   c. How is the benefit plan funded?
    i. Funded plan--employer makes periodic payments to an independent funding agent.
    ii. Unfunded plan--employer retains control of the benefit plan funds.

IV. Balanced scorecard approach translates a company's strategy into objectives and plans.
 A. The balanced scorecard has four perspectives.
  1. Financial perspective--profits are necessary to remain attractive to investors and creditors.
   a. Measures include net income, financial ratios, and return on investment (ROI).
  2. Internal process perspective--seeks to find measures of improvement in the way work is done and the manner in which people are utilized in the company.
   a. Uses measures related to quality, supplier relationships, on-time deliveries to customers, innovation, employee satisfaction, employee retention, and employee productivity.
  3. Customer perspective--relates to managing the company's customer base.
   a. Measures are linked to strategies to increase market share, to acquire more or larger customers, and by increasing customer satisfaction.
  4. Learning and growth perspective--involves managing the company's future.

        a. Focuses on research and development activities, educating and cross-training employees, measuring investments in technology, and improving business processes.
    B. The balanced scorecard approach may be used in the employee reward system.
       1. The approach does not suggest that financial measures be abandoned; it suggests that other measures of performance should be included in the evaluation and reward process.
       2. Helps reduce goal incongruence (when an employee's and company's goals for the future are not aligned).

V. (Appendix) Motivation and leadership theories affect reward systems.
    A. Maslow's hierarchy of needs states when needs at the lower level are met, they are no longer motivational.
       1. The needs from lowest to highest are:
          a. Physical needs.
          b. Safety.
          c. Belongingness.
          d. Esteem.
          e. Self-actualization.
    B. Herzberg's motivation theory divides needs into two categories.
         a. Hygiene factors--do not motivate; but if they are absent or poorly delivered, decreased motivation occurs.
         b. Motivator factors--when increased do lead to increased motivation.
    C. Vroom's expectancy theory relates a person's motivation to the importance he or she places on, or the desire to achieve, certain outcomes and the person's expectation that a given level of effort will result in the achievement of the outcome.
    D. McGregor's theory of leadership states that managers have two different attitudes toward employees that result in two different leadership styles.
       1. Theory X--employees are lazy, must be coerced to work, and strive to avoid responsibility.
          a. Manager will closely supervise employees, use threats to motivate, and will not delegate authority or responsibility.
       2. Theory Y--people like work, will work toward goals laid out for them, and will commit to goals that are rewarded.
          a. Manager will loosely supervise employees, allow employees to set their own goals, and will reward employees for achievement and creativity.
    E. Power is a source of leadership.
       1. Expert power--perception that the manager is the most competent person or has the best knowledge base in the situation.
       2. Legitimate power--results from the manager's position in the company hierarchy.
       3. Reward power--results from the ability of the manger to grant rewards to employees.
       4. Coercive power--results from the manager's ability to punish employees.

©The McGraw-Hill Companies, Inc., 2000

Problem I

Indicate whether the following statements are either true (T) or false (F).

_____1. An employee's expected future benefit to the company will be shown as an asset on the balance sheet.
_____2. Contributory plans are funded either partially or totally by employees' contributions.
_____3. The learning and growth perspective is closely related to the internal perspective.
_____4. An organic organizational structure is often found when the company is operating in a certain external environment.
_____5. Bonuses are forms of compensation contingent on the occurrence of some specified future event.
_____6. In an unvested plan, employees have no rights to the benefit plan when employment ceases.
_____7. A company's largest noncapitalized asset is its customer base.
_____8. Under piece-rate pay, employee compensation is based on the number of items completed.
_____9. Companies adopting a flexible organizational strategy focus on cost containment.
_____10. When hourly pay is used, compensation is independent of the amount of work completed.
_____11. Under a certain external environment, cost control becomes the primary concern of management.
_____12. The most common form of compensation is commission pay.

Problem II

Indicate the correct answer by circling the appropriate letter.

1. Which of the following statements is true for a company operating in an uncertain external environment?
    a. Companies concentrate on customer satisfaction.
    b. Companies concentrate on new product development.
    c. The companies often have an organic organizational structure.
    d. All of the above are true.

2. Companies adopting a flexibility strategy with respect to human resource management, tend to _____.
    a. staff externally
    b. use job-specific training
    c. build skills needed
    d. all of the above are consistent with a flexibility strategy

3. A pension plan will generally describe _____.
   a. who will pay for the pension benefits
   b. how the money contributed to the pension plan will be invested
   c. how and when the benefits will be paid to the employee
   d. all of the above

4. Which of the following will not affect the pension benefit received under a defined contribution plan?
   a. The net income earned by the company.
   b. The contributions rate.
   c. Years worked by the employee.
   d. The return earned on the funds invested by the trustee.

5. Richie Rich is paid a bonus equal to 3 percent of income before taxes. If the company's income before taxes and the bonus was $3,000,000, Richie's bonus will be _____.
   a. $90,000
   b. $83,600
   c. $87,389
   d. $91,348

6. A post-retirement benefit plan where the employee has rights to the benefits even if not employed at the time, is called a (an) _____ plan.
   a. vested plan
   b. unvested plan
   c. bonus plan
   d. funded plan

7. A structure in which activities and employees are arranged by cross-functional teams is called a (an) _____.
   a. mechanistic organizational structure
   b. holistic organizational structure
   c. organic organizational structure
   d. variant organizational structure

8. Which of the following is not true about compensation in the form of salary pay?
   a. The amount is fixed per pay period.
   b. The amount of pay is independent of the hours worked.
   c. The amount of pay is independent of the amount of work completed.
   d. The amount is usually based on the amount of revenue generated.

9. Mary Minter receives a bonus each year equal to 6 percent of income before income taxes. During the year, the company reported income before taxes (and the bonus) of $600,000. The company's effective income tax rate is 40 percent. What will Mary receive as a bonus for the year?
   a. $36,000
   b. $21,600
   c. $32,841
   d. $33,962

10. Which of the following is a benefit of a stock option plan.
    a. No current cash outflow to the company.
    b. Company saves on recruiting, training, and employee development costs.
    c. Generally, no expense is recognized by the company.
    d. All are potential benefits of a stock option plan.

11. Which of the following is not used to monitor/measure the learning and growth perspective?
    a. number of new products introduced
    b. number of employees trained
    c. investments in information technology
    d. employee turnover

Problem III

Following is a list of important ideas and key concepts from the chapter. To test your knowledge of these terms, match the term with the definition by placing the number in the space provided.

_____ bonus base
_____ commission pay
_____ contributory plan
_____ defined benefit plan
_____ defined contribution plan
_____ efficiency strategy

_____ flexibility strategy
_____ goal incongruence
_____ noncontributory plan
_____ organizational strategy
_____ unfunded plan
_____ vested plan

1. A strategy focuses primarily on the reduction or containment of costs, improvements in productivity, and penetration of products and services having low cost

2. A post-retirement benefit plan where the employee has rights to the benefits even if the employee is not employed at the time

3. Compensation based on the percentage of revenue generated

4. A strategy focused primarily on adapting the changing conditions by expanding (or contracting) product lines, customer bases, and markets

5. A post-retirement benefit plan where the employer promises to make specific contributions to the plan, but the post-retirement benefits received by retirees are not specified

6. A post-retirement benefit plan where the employer retains control of the benefit plan funds

7. The form of income the bonus rate is applied to

8. A post-retirement benefit plan where both the employee and employer contribute

9. A post-retirement benefit plan where only the employer contributes to the plan

10. A post-retirement benefit plan where the employer promises to pay retirees a specified amount at retirement, but the contributions made to the plan are not specified

11. A situation in which an employee's goals and the company's goals are not aligned

12. A company's long-term plan for using its resources

Problem IV

Complete the following sentences by filling in the correct response.

1. _____ is the set of policies and procedures companies use to ensure effective and efficient use of their human capital.

2. Group health insurance rates will typically be _____ than individual rates.

3. Pension _____ is the act of making contributions to the pension plan.

4. Defined contribution plans specify the _____ to be contributed whereas defined benefit plans specify the _____ to be paid at retirement.

5. The external environment can be considered a continuum with _____ at one end and _____ at the other end.

6. _____ and _____ _____ are used by a company to get employees to accept some of the business risk.

©The McGraw-Hill Companies, Inc., 2000

7. An organization's strategy is a function of its _____ environment and its _____ structure.

8. Companies adopting a flexibility strategy strive to adapt to changing _____ conditions by expanding (or contracting) _____ lines.

9. Commission pay is usually based on _____ or _____.

10. Internally, the most widely used measure of performance is _____.

11. To increase customer satisfaction, the company must add value by providing _____ and _____.

Problem V

Albert, age 30, is an employee of Aceway Inc. which maintains a defined benefit plan. Albert plans to retire at age 50 and has a life expectancy of 75. Albert wants to receive $50,000 a year at retirement. Prior to retirement, the pension plan is expected to earn 12 percent on all investments. At retirement, the company plans to purchase an annuity to pay the $50,000 annual retirement payment. The annuity will earn 6 percent during Albert's life.

1. How much money must the company have accumulated by the time of Albert's retirement?

2. What will be the cost of the company's annual funding related to Albert's postretirement benefit?

60

Study Guide, Introduction to Accounting: An Integrated Approach

Problem VI

1. Human resource management begins with the planning process. List the four steps used in human resource planning.

_____
_____
_____
_____

2. Describe costs that are often incurred in a human resource department of a company.

_____
_____
_____
_____
_____
_____
_____
_____
_____

3. What are the benefits of good employee recruitment and selection strategy?

_____
_____
_____
_____
_____
_____
_____
_____

4. List three criteria that companies use to monitor the customer perspective.

_____
_____
_____
_____
_____
_____

Problem VII

Use the following information to calculate the bonus under the assumptions given:

    Income before income taxes $2,200,000
    Effective income tax rate   35%
    Bonus rate   5%

1. The bonus is based on income before the bonus or income taxes.

2. The bonus is based on income before income taxes.

3. The bonus is based on net income.

Pause and Reflect

Present GAAP does not allow the reporting of employees as assets. However, many European and a growing number of U.S. corporations are disclosing information about employees in their annual reports. What types of information do you think would be disclosed and why?

Solutions for Chapter 16

Problem I

1. F
2. T
3. T
4. F
5. T
6. T
7. T
8. T
9. F
10. T
11. T
12. F

Problem II

1. d
2. a
3. d
4. a
5. c
6. a
7. c
8. d
9. d
10. d
11. d

Problem III

7 bonus base
3 commission pay
8 contributory plan
10 defined benefit plan
5 defined contribution plan
1 efficiency strategy

4 flexibility strategy
11 goal incongruence
9 noncontributory plan
12 organizational strategy
6 unfunded plan
2 vested plan

Study Guide, Introduction to Accounting: An Integrated Approach

Problem IV

1. Human resource management
2. lower
3. funding
4. amount, benefit
5. certainty, uncertainty
6. Bonuses, stock options
7. external, organizational
8. market, product
9. net sales, contribution margin
10. return on investment
11. quality, reliability

Problem V

1. The company must accumulate the present value of a $50,000 annuity over Albert's life expectancy at retirement.

   Pva(25, 6%) X $50,000 = 12.7834 X $50,000 = $639,170

2. The cost of the company's annual funding will be the annuity payment necessary to accumulate $639,170 at Albert's retirement date.

   Fva(20, 12%) X Annuity Pmt = $639,170

   72.0524 X Annuity Pmt = $639,170

   Annuity Pmt = $8,871

Problem VI

1. a. Determine job skills needed in the future
   b. Assess the skills of the current workforce
   c. Determine the future supply of human capital
   d. Prepare a strategic plan for obtaining human capital

2. a. salaries paid to human resource employees
    b. costs of advertising for positions
    c. travel costs incurred to interview potential employees
    d. recordkeeping costs for employee files
    e. recordkeeping costs to indicate compliance with regulations
    f. costs incurred for background investigations of potential employees

3. A good recruitment and selection strategy minimizes the chance of hiring incompetent or unproductive employees, reduces the chances of labor-related litigation and helps insure a good fit between the employee and company which will result in a long-term cost savings to the company.

4. a. number of new customers acquired
    b. the amount of profit generated by new customers
    c. the growth in market share

Problem VII

1. $2,200,000 \times .05 = \$110,000$

2. $(\$2,200,000 - B) \times .05 = B$
   $\$110,000 - .05B = B$
   $\$110,000 = 1.05B$
   Bonus = $104,762

3. $B = (\$2,200,000 - B - T) \times .05$

   $T = (\$2,200,000 - B) \times .35$
   $T = \$770,000 - .35B$

   $B = (\$2,200,000 - B - \$770,000 + .35B) \times .05$
   $B = \$71,500 - .0325B$
   $1.0325B = \$71,500$
   Bonus = $69,249

Pause and Reflect

European companies often report information about age and seniority, training, fringe benefits, and absenteeism. U.S. firms, such as Ford Motor Company, may report information about the number of employees by geographic area and the number of minority group members and women employed. Employee disclosures reflect the viewpoint that a company's continued success depends in part on its employees, or human resources.

Chapter 17
Planning for Equity Financing

Chapter Overview

Chapter 17 investigates equity financing as a means of raising the capital necessary to run the business and invest in long-term projects. The chapter explores the partnership and corporate forms of equity financing. Terms related to the corporate form of equity financing are discussed in depth. The characteristics of both partnerships and corporate equity instruments are presented. In addition, the chapter discusses the costs and benefits of equity financing versus debt financing.

As you study this chapter, it will be necessary to learn the terms associated with both partnership and corporate forms of equity financing. You should be able to identify the advantages and disadvantages of both of these equity-financing options. In a later chapter you will study how to record and communicate the results of equity financing activities. Therefore, you will be asked to apply what you learn in this chapter to the recording of these activities in the accounting system.

Read and Recall Questions

Learning Objective:
L.O.1. Explain the risks and rewards of equity financing.

What are the three ways a firm may acquire funds?

Distinguish between equity financing and debt financing.

What rewards do owners receive for committing their resources to the enterprise? What risks do the owners of a business face?

What are the three basic forms of business ownership?

What are the three important advantages of sole proprietorships and partnerships? What are the two disadvantages?

What are the three advantages of the corporate form of business ownership? What are two disadvantages of corporations?

Learning Objective:
L.O.2. Describe the characteristics of partnerships.

If a partnership agreement does not specify how profits and losses are shared, how are the profits and losses divided?

What are five common methods for dividing partnership earnings?

If a partnership agreement specifies how profits are divided but not losses, how are the losses divided among partners? Is it possible for some partners' capital accounts to increase even when the partnership incurs a loss? Explain.

In what two ways may a new partner be admitted to a partnership?

What effect does the purchase of an existing interest have on the assets of the partnership? What is the effect on the partners' capital accounts?

When a new partner makes a direct investment in the firm, a bonus may be paid to the existing partners. What situation results in the payment of a bonus to existing partners?

When a new partner makes a direct investment in the firm, a bonus may be given to the new partner. What situation results in giving a bonus to the new partner?

Why do firms usually revalue assets before admitting a new partner?

What are three ways a partner may withdraw from a partnership?

> **Learning Objective:**
> L.O.3. Describe the characteristics of corporate equity instruments.

What is common stock? What rights of ownership are associated with common stock?

What is preferred stock? What preferences do preferred stockholders receive? What rights do preferred stockholders usually give up?

What is cumulative preferred stock? What are dividends in arrears?

What is participating preferred stock?

Distinguish among callable preferred stock, redeemable preferred stock, and convertible preferred stock.

Distinguish among authorized shares, issued shares, and outstanding shares.

What is treasury stock? What is the effect of treasury stock on stockholders' equity?

Why do corporations buy treasury stock?

Define par value. What is paid-in capital in excess of par?

What is a legal capital?

What is the difference between no-par stock and no-par, stated value stock?

What is the market value of a share of stock? What causes the market value of a share of stock to increase or decrease?

What are dividends? What are liquidating dividends?

What is a stock dividend? Why would a corporation issue a stock dividend rather than a cash dividend?

What are the four dates related to dividends?

What is a stock split? What happens to each stockholder's ownership percentage as a result of a stock split? What happens to the total par value of the shares issued?

Why do companies enter into stock splits?

Where do companies find equity financing?

Outline of Key Concepts

I. Funds may be acquired through two financing categories.
   A. Equity financing--a means for firms to obtain funds in exchange for an ownership interest in the firm.
      1. Through contribution of assets to the firm by investors.
      2. Through reinvestment of the firm's earnings.
   B. Debt financing--when a company obtains funds in exchange for a liability to repay the borrowed funds.

II. Rewards and risks of equity financing.
   A. Rewards include a satisfactory return on the initial investment and the psychological rewards of ownership.
   B. Risks include not receiving a satisfactory return on invested funds or losing some or all of the investment.
      1. In general, the greater the debt the firm incurs, the greater the risk to the owners.

III. Business ownership structures have unique advantages and disadvantages.
   A. Sole proprietorships and partnerships have three advantages.
      1. Ease of formation.
      2. Income generated by the sole proprietorship or partnership is taxed only once.
      3. Owners are more likely to manage the business and be involved in its operation.
   B. Sole proprietorships and partnerships have two disadvantages.
      1. Unlimited liability--owners can lose not only what they have invested but also their personal assets when the assets of the firm do not satisfy the creditors' claims.
      2. Inability to raise large amounts of equity capital.
   C. Corporations have three major advantages.
      1. Limited liability--owners can lose only the amounts invested in the firm.
      2. Ability to raise large amounts of capital by selling its stock.
      3. Unlimited life.
   D. Corporations have two disadvantages.
      1. Time and cost to become incorporated and satisfy the regulatory requirements.

2. Double taxation--the corporation's profits are taxed at the corporate level and again when they are distributed to the owners in the form of dividends.

IV. Planning for partnership equity.
   A. The income or loss generated by the partnership during the period is allocated to the partners, resulting in an increase or decrease to the respective partners' capital accounts.
      1. Commonly used methods for dividing earnings include:
         a. Fixed ratios.
         b. Ratio of capital account balances.
            i. Partners must decide whether the ratio is based on beginning, ending, or average balances.
         c. Salary allowances and some determination of distribution of any remainder.
            i. Allocates earnings on the basis of the amount of time each partner spends operating the business.
            ii. The salary allowance is not considered an expense of the business.
         d. Interest allowance on capital balances and some determination of distribution of any remainder.
            i. Designed to reward partners who invest and maintain capital in the business.
            ii. Agreement must specify interest rate and which balances to use.
         e. Combination of salary and interest allowance.
      2. In the absence of an agreement to the contrary, the law provides that partners share profits and losses equally.
   B. Admitting a new partner dissolves the old partnership and creates a new partnership.
      1. New partner may purchase all or part of the interest of an existing partner by payment to the existing partner.
         a. New partner receives all or a portion of the selling partner's capital.
         b. This transaction does not change the amount of the firm's assets.
      2. New partner may invest directly in the partnership organization.
         a. The payment of cash or other assets increases the amount of the firm's total assets as well as its total owners' equity.
         b. The new partner's interest in the firm can be the same, smaller, or larger than the amount of the assets contributed.
         c. If a new partner is required to pay a price greater than the amount credited to his or her capital account, the excess payment is viewed as a bonus to the existing partners.
         d. If a new partner receives a capital credit greater than the price paid, the excess capital credit is a bonus to the new partner.
      3. The partnership may revalue its assets before admitting a new partner if the partnership structure has not changed for an extended period of time or when asset values have changed substantially.
   C. A partner's withdrawal may occur in one of three ways.

©The McGraw-Hill Companies, Inc., 2000

1. His or her interest may be purchased by one or more of the remaining partners.
   a. On the partnership books, this involves an exchange of capital only.
2. His or her interest may be purchased by an outsider seeking admission to the partnership.
   a. For the partnership, this involves an exchange of capital only.
3. His or her interest may be purchased by the partnership itself.
   a. The amount paid may equal, exceed, or be less than the balance in the withdrawing partner's capital account.

V. Equity instruments are used to indicate ownership.
   A. Common stock represents the basic ownership unit of the corporation.
      1. Common stockholders normally have the following rights: right to vote, the right to dividends, the right to residual assets upon liquidation of the corporation, the right to dispose of the shares by sale or gift, and the preemptive right.
         a. Preemptive right--the right to maintain the percentage ownership interest in the corporation when it issues new shares of stock.
      2. Common stock represents the residual ownership interest.
   B. Preferred stock represents an ownership interest in a corporation with special privileges or preferences as to liquidation and dividends.
      1. The preference is in reference to common stockholders.
      2. Preferred stockholders usually give up voting rights.
      3. There are five basic types of preferred stock.
         a. Cumulative preferred stock--accumulates dividends over time if the corporation does not pay them in full when stipulated.
            i. Dividends in arrears--preferred stock dividends that were not paid when stipulated.
         b. Participating preferred stock--allows preferred stockholders the right to receive an amount in excess of the stated dividend rate or amount.
         c. Callable preferred stock--gives the corporation the right to repurchase the preferred stock at a stipulated price.
         d. Redeemable preferred stock--gives the stockholder the right to turn in the stock for cash at the stockholder's option.
         e. Convertible preferred stock--gives stockholders the right to convert (exchange) preferred shares for other forms of capital at the option of the preferred stockholder.
   C. How many shares are there?
      1. Shares authorized--the total number of shares the state has approved for a corporation to sell.
      2. Shares issued--the number of authorized shares a corporation has sold to stockholders.
      3. Outstanding shares--the number of shares issued and held by stockholders.
      4. Treasury stock--the amount of a corporation's repurchased stock that it intends to reissue at a later date.
         a. The corporation is not buying an asset; it is reducing its stockholders' equity.

D. Capital stock has several values.
   1. Par value--an arbitrary value assigned to shares of capital stock as approved by the state in which the business is incorporated.
      a. Legal capital--the portion of stockholders' equity required by state law to be retained for the protection of the corporation's creditors.
      b. Paid-in capital in excess of par--the amount received from stock issuance in excess of the par value of the stock.
   2. No-par value--no minimum price assigned to each share of stock.
      a. No-par, stated value stock--has a minimum price or stated value established by the corporation's board of directors but no par value specified in the state charter.
   3. Market value--the price agreed to by an unrelated willing buyer and seller.
E. Dividends--a distribution of the assets of the corporation to the owners of the corporation.
   1. Dividends may be in the form of cash, additional shares of stock, or property.
   2. There are four dates related to dividends.
      a. Date of declaration--date on which the board of directors announces its decision to pay a dividend to stockholders.
      b. Date of record--date on which the secretary of the corporation determines who is officially registered as a stockholder of the corporation.
      c. Ex-dividend date--occur two or three days prior to the date of record and is the last date when an individual can buy the stock of the corporation and still receive the declared dividend.
      d. Date of payment--date on which the company formally pays the dividend to stockholders of record.
F. Stock splits--occur when a corporation calls in its old shares of stock and issues a larger number of new shares of stock in their place.
   1. Each stockholder retains the same percentage ownership interest in the corporation.
   2. The par or stated value of the stock also reflects the change.
   3. Companies use stock splits to lower the market price of their stock to allow the price to be affordable to a wider group of potential investors.
G. Where do corporations find equity financing?
   1. Smaller businesses may sell stock directly to persons who have an interest in the business.
   2. Larger companies use investment bankers to find buyers for their stock.

Problem I

Indicate whether the following statements are either true (T) or false (F).

____ 1. Reinvestment of a company's earnings is considered equity financing.
____ 2. The risk to owners of a corporation is limited to the amount invested.
____ 3. Callable preferred stock gives the shareholder the right to turn in the stock for cash at the stockholder's option.
____ 4. Par value of stock is the price agreed to by an unrelated willing buyer and seller.
____ 5. A stock dividend will not change an investor's percentage ownership interest in the corporation.
____ 6. Partners have unlimited liability for the debts of the partnership.
____ 7. Corporations are subject to double taxation.
____ 8. In absence of an agreement to the contrary, partners will share profits and losses in the same ratio as their capital contributions.
____ 9. Admission of a new partner will not cause the old partnership to be dissolved.
____ 10. Outstanding shares are the number of shares issued less the number of shares repurchased and held as treasury stock.

Problem II

Indicate the correct answer by circling the appropriate letter.

1. Which of the following is not a right normally associated with the ownership of common stock?
   a. Preference over creditors to assets in liquidation.
   b. Preemptive right.
   c. Right to vote on significant events that affect the corporation
   d. All of the above are rights of a common stock shareholder.

2. X Corporation will issue 500,000 shares of additional common stock on December 1. Janet currently owns 2% of X Corporation's outstanding stock. Janet has the first option to purchase _____ shares of the stock.
   a. - 0 -
   b. 10,000
   c. 100,000
   d. 500,000

3. Preferred stock shareholders will generally have which of the following rights?
    a. Right to receive dividends before common stock shareholders.
    b. Right to assets in liquidation before common stock shareholders.
    c. Right to assets in liquidation before creditors.
    d. Both a and b.

4. Y Corporation has 10,000 shares of $5, noncumulative, $100 par, preferred stock outstanding. If a dividend is declared, what amount will preferred stock shareholders receive before common stock shareholders receive any dividend?
    a. $50,000
    b. $100,000
    c. $250,000
    d. none of the above

5. Z Corporation has cumulative preferred stock outstanding that carries a normal dividend of $200,000. The corporation is 3 years in arrears on dividend payments. What amount will common stock shareholders receive if a $1,000,000 dividend is paid in the current year?
    a. - 0 -
    b. $200,000
    c. $400,000
    d. $800,000

6. With respect to a cash dividend, a legal liability (obligation) is created on the following date:
    a. The date of declaration
    b. The date of record
    c. The ex-dividend date
    d. Date of payment

7. Which of the following is not an advantage of a sole proprietorship or partnership.
    a. limited liability
    b. ease of formation
    c. income is only taxed once
    d. none of the above is an advantage of a sole proprietorship or partnership

8. Jack, Jerry and Jane formed a partnership and agreed to share profits in a fixed ratio of 3:2:1, respectively. If the partnership earned $36,000 during the year, Jack's capital account will be increased by _____.
    a. $6,000
    b. $12,000
    c. $18,000
    d. $36,000

9. The M&M Partnership is owned by Max and Mary. Since Mary will manage daily operations, she receives a salary allocation of $35,000 each year. Any remaining profits or losses are shared equally. M&M reported net income of $25,000 for the year. Mary's capital account will increase by _____.
   a. $17,500
   b. $30,000
   c. $35,000
   d. $40,000

10. Which of the following is not an advantage of a corporation.
    a. limited liability
    b. ability to raise large amounts of money
    c. unlimited life
    d. income only taxed once

Problem III

Following is a list of important ideas and key concepts from the chapter. To test your knowledge of these terms, match the term with the definition by placing the number in the space provided.

_____ authorized shares   _____ legal capital
_____ callable preferred stock   _____ par value
_____ common stock   _____ participating preferred stock
_____ convertible preferred stock   _____ preemptive right
_____ cumulative preferred stock   _____ retired shares
_____ date of payment   _____ stock dividend
_____ dividends in arrears   _____ stock split
_____ ex-dividend date   _____ treasury stock

1. The shares of a corporation's issued stock that the corporation has repurchased and intends to reissue at a later date

2. The amount of cumulative preferred stock dividends not paid in full when stipulated

3. A right of common stockholders that allows them to maintain their percentage interest in the corporation when it issues new shares of common stock

4. The last date when an individual can buy the stock of the corporation and still receive the corporation's declared dividend

5. Repurchased issued shares that the corporation will never reissue

6. Preferred stock that gives the issuing corporation the right to repurchased the preferred stock at a stipulated price

7. The total number of shares the state has approved for a corporation to sell

8. The distribution of additional shares of the corporation's stock to existing stockholders

9. The basic ownership unit of a corporation

10. The date on which the corporation formally pays dividends to stockholders of record

11. The portion of stockholders' equity required by state law to be retained for the protection of the corporation's creditors

12. Preferred stock that gives the stockholder the right to convert (exchange) the preferred shares for other forms of capital, as stated in the corporate charter, at the option of the preferred stockholder

13. Preferred stock that allows preferred stockholders the right to receive an amount in excess of the stated dividend rate or amount

14. The corporation's recall of its old shares of stock and issuance of a larger number of new shares in their place

15. Preferred stock that accumulates dividends over time if the corporation does not pay them in full when stipulated

16. An arbitrary value assigned to shares of capital stock which is approved by the state in which the business is incorporated

©The McGraw-Hill Companies, Inc., 2000

Problem IV

Complete the following sentences by filling in the correct response.

1. _____ stock represents the basic ownership unit of the corporation.

2. The _____ right allows common stock shareholders to maintain their percentage ownership interest in a corporation.

3. _____ preferred stock indicates the corporation has the right to repurchase the stock at a predetermined price.

4. The portion of stockholders' equity required by state law to be retained for the protection of the corporation's creditors is referred to as _____ _____.

5. _____ are distributions of assets of the corporation to shareholders and typically are made from the _____ of the company.

6. A _____ dividend is the distribution of non-cash assets to the stockholders of a company.

7. When a company obtains funds in exchange for a liability to repay the borrowed funds it is referred to as _____ financing.

8. When a company obtains funds in exchange for an ownership interest in the firm it is referred to as _____ financing.

Problem V

The average capital balances for ABC Partnership are provided below:

A, capital	$50,000
B, capital	$40,000
C, capital	$10,000

Allocate the current period's net income of $80,000 under each of the allocation agreements below:

1. Income and losses are allocated in the ration of 4:3:1.

2. Income and losses are allocated in the ratio of the capital account balances.

3. A is to receive a salary of $30,000 with remaining profits allocated in the ratio of the capital account balances.

4. Interest of 6 percent is paid on the average capital account balance with remaining profits and losses shared in a ratio of 3:2:1.

Problem VI

The partnership of Andrews, Jones and Kim had the following capital balances:

	Balance	Ownership Percent
Andrews	$40,000	50%
Jones	$20,000	25%
Kim	$20,000	25%

Profits are shared in proportion to each partner's capital balance.

The partners have agreed to admit Fox to the partnership. Calculate each partner's capital balance after admission of Fox under the following alternatives:

1. Fox will purchase Andrew's partnership interest for $50,000.

2. Fox will be admitted to the partnership by contributing $20,000 for a 10 percent ownership interest.

3. Fox will be admitted to the partnership by contributing $16,000 for a 20 percent ownership interest.

Solutions for Chapter 17

Problem I

1. T
2. T
3. F
4. F
5. T
6. T
7. T
8. F
9. F
10. T

Problem II

1. a
2. b
3. d
4. a
5. b
6. a
7. a
8. c
9. b
10. d

Problem III

7	authorized shares	11	legal capital
6	callable preferred stock	16	par value
9	common stock	13	participating preferred stock
12	convertible preferred stock	3	preemptive right
15	cumulative preferred stock	5	retired shares
10	date of payment	8	stock dividend
2	dividends in arrears	14	stock split
4	ex-dividend date	1	treasury stock

Problem IV

1. Common
2. preemptive
3. Callable
4. legal capital
5. Dividends, earnings
6. property
7. debt
8. equity

Problem V

1. A 4/8 X $80,000 = $40,000
   B 3/8 X $80,000 = $30,000
   C 1/8 X $80,000 = $10,000

2. A $50,000/$100,000 X $80,000 = $40,000
   B $40,000/$100,000 X $80,000 = $32,000
   C $10,000/$100,000 X $80,000 = $ 8,000

3.

Item	A	B	C	Amount Distributed	Amount Remaining
Net income					$80,000
Salary Allowance	$30,000	$ - 0 -	$ - 0 -	$30,000	50,000
Remainder	25,000	20,000	5,000	50,000	- 0 -
	$55,000	$20,000	$5,000	$80,000	- 0 -

4. Interest Allocation:
   A $ 50,000 X .06 = $3,000
   B $ 40,000 X .06 = $2,400
   C $ 10,000 X .06 = $ 600
   Total $100,000 X .06 = $6,000

Item	A	B	C	Amount Distributed	Amount Remaining
Net income					$80,000
Interest Allowance	$ 3,000	$ 2,400	$ 600	$ 6,000	74,000
Remainder	37,000	24,667	12,333	74,000	- 0 -
	$40,000	$27,067	$12,933	$80,000	- 0 -

Problem VI

1. Jones, capital $20,000
   Kim, capital $20,000
   Fox, capital $40,000

2. Andrews, capital $40,000 + (.50 X $10,000) = $45,000
   Jones, capital $20,000 + (.25 X $10,000) = $22,500
   Kim, capital $20,000 + (.25 X $10,000) = $22,500
   Fox, capital $10,000

       Fox   .10 X ($40,000 + $20,000 + $20,000 + $20,000) = $10,000

       Bonus to existing partners $20,000 - $10,000 = $10,000

3. Andrews, capital $40,000 - (.50 X $3,200) = $38,400
   Jones, capital $20,000 - (.25 X $3,200) = $19,200
   Kim, capital $20,000 - (.25 X $3,200) = $19,200
   Fox, capital $19,200

       Fox   .20 X ($40,000 + $20,000 + $20,000 + $16,000) = $19,200

       Bonus to Fox $19,200 - $16,000 = $3,200

Chapter 18
Planning for Debt Financing

Chapter Overview

Chapter 18 explores the use of debt financing to raise the capital necessary to operate a business and to enable a business to invest in long-term projects. The chapter illustrates how the use of debt financing creates the potential for increasing the owners' return on investment. This effect is referred to as financial leverage. The chapter describes the types of promissory notes and explains how they work. The chapter concludes by examining financing plans. These plans project the impact that proposed financing alternatives will have on cash flows, income, and financial position.

As in previous chapters, it is necessary that you become familiar with the new terms presented. You will be drawing upon your knowledge of the time value of money once again. Present value calculations are an integral part of determining the issue price of bonds and recognizing interest expense. If needed, you may wish to review Chapter 14 as you study this chapter. In addition to understanding the calculations presented, you should develop an understanding of the potential benefits of debt financing versus equity financing. Conceptually, you should try to link Chapters 17 and 18 together as alternative approaches in the process of raising capital for running the business.

Read and Recall Questions

> **Learning Objective:**
> L.O.1. Explain the risks and reward of long-term debt financing.

What is debt financing? Why do firms use long-term liabilities?

What is financial risk? What may happen if a firm defaults on its debt?

What is financial leverage? How may it benefit the owners of the firm?

What is the rate of return on owners' equity (ROE)? How is it calculated?

What does the debt-to-equity ratio measure? How is it calculated?

How does one know what an appropriate debt-to-equity ratio would be?

What does the times interest earned ratio measure? How is it calculated?

What are the indicators that a firm has greater financial risk than another firm?

Learning Objective:
L.O.2. Describe the characteristics of the three basic types of long-term debt instruments.

Why may lenders place covenants on the borrowings of a company?

Distinguish between the face value and proceeds of a note.

Distinguish between the face rate and market or effective interest rate. Why may the market rate differ from the face rate?

What is a periodic payment or installment note?

What is an amortization table?

What is a lump-sum payment note? Why are these notes often called noninterest-bearing notes?

What determines the face value of a noninterest-bearing note?

What does the discount on a note represent?

What is the carrying value of a note?

How is the interest expense on a noninterest-bearing note determined?

What is a periodic payment and lump-sum note? Why is it often referred to as an interest-bearing note?

What determines the amount of proceeds that a borrower will receive on an interest-bearing note?

What does it mean when an interest-bearing note is issued at a discount? What is the impact of a discount on interest expense?

What are the steps for determining the proceeds of an interest-bearing note issued at a discount? Which interest rate, face or market, is used to calculate the proceeds?

What does it mean when an interest-bearing note is issued at a premium? What is the impact of a premium on interest expense?

When the market rate is equal to the face rate of interest, will the proceeds of the note be the same as, less than, or greater than the face value of the note? Explain.

Learning Objective:
L.O.3. Identify sources of debt financing.

How does nonpublic debt financing occur?

What is collateral? A mortgage?

What is a lease? Distinguish between an operating lease and a capital lease.

How is a capital lease reported in the financial statements?

What are bonds? Why do corporations issue bonds?

How can the sale of bonds be handled?

If a $5,000 bond is listed at 97.5 on the secondary bond market, what is the sales price of the bond?

What is the difference between registered bonds and bearer bonds?

Distinguish between callable bonds and convertible bonds. What is a serial bond?

What is the purpose of the security feature of a secured bond?

What are subordinated bonds?

Learning Objective:
L.O.4. Understand how firms plan their financial structure.

What are pro forma financial statements? How can these statements be used to choose between debt and equity financing?

Which ratios should be analyzed when choosing between debt and equity financing?

If a project will have minimal positive cash during the first few years, what type of note should the project managers consider using for debt financing? Why?

When selecting a debt instrument, planners should consider the instrument's impact on the income statement, balance sheet, and cash flows statement. Which of these statements should be the most important factor? Why?

Outline of Key Concepts

I. Debt financing occurs when a firm incurs a liability in the process of acquiring goods or services.
    A. Risks and rewards of debt financing.
        1. Financial risk--the chance that a firm will default on its debt.
        2. The reward for debt financing occurs when companies generate a return on their borrowed funds that is greater than the cost to them of using the borrowed funds.
    B. Financial leverage--a financing strategy designed to increase the rate of return on owners' investment by generating a greater return on borrowed funds than the cost of using the funds.
        1. Return on owners' equity (ROE)--measures the performance of the firm in terms of the owners' investment.
            a. ROE = Net income/Owners' equity
        2. Debt-to-equity ratio--measures the relationship between the amount of debt and the amount of owners' equity used to finance the firm.
            a. Debt-to-equity ratio = Total debt/Stockholders' equity
            b. The larger the debt-to-equity ratio, the greater the amount of debt used to finance the firm and, therefore, the greater the financial risk.
            c. Sales volatility can increase financial risk.
        3. Times interest earned ratio--measures a firm's ability to service its debt.

a. Times interest earned ratio = Earnings before interest and taxes/Interest expense

II. Long-term debt instruments are promises of the firms that borrow money.
   A. General terms associated with long-term debt include the following.
      1. Covenants--restrictions placed on companies by lenders.
      2. Face value of the note--indicates the amount that the maker of the note will ultimately pay the holder of the note.
      3. Face rate of the note--determines the amount of cash interest the maker will pay the holder of the note.
      4. Proceeds--the amount of cash raised from the issuance of the debt.
      5. Market or effect interest rate--the actual interest rate charged for the use of the proceeds of the note.
   B. There are three types of notes.
      1. Periodic payment note--a debt instrument that contains a promise to make a series of equal payments consisting of both interest and principal at equal time intervals over a specified time period.
         a. Usually called an installment note.
      2. Lump-sum payment note--a debt instrument that contains a promise to pay a specific amount of money at the end of the specific period of time.
         a. Often called a noninterest-bearing note because the note only specifies a face value and a due date.
         b. Amount of cash loaned is the present value of the face value at some market rate of interest.
         c. Discount on a note--dollar difference between the face value of the note and the cash proceeds received.
            i. Discount will be amortized over the life of the note.
         d. Carrying value--face value minus the discount.
      3. Periodic payment and lump-sum note-- has a face rate of interest and a face value and the maker promises to make periodic cash interest payments and a lump-sum payment on the date the note matures.
         a. When the market rate of interest is greater than the face rate of interest, the proceeds of the note are less than the face value of the note.
            i. Note is issued at a discount to make the note yield the market rate of interest.
            ii. The discount is actually additional interest that will be paid over the life of the note.
            iii. Cash interest is based on the face interest rate times the face value, while the effective interest is the market rate of interest of the note times the carrying value of the note.
         b. When the market rate of interest is less than the face rate of interest on the note, the proceeds of the note are greater than the face value of the note.

        i.   Note is issued at a premium to make the note yield the market rate of interest.
        ii.   The premium will reduce the amount of interest expense over the life of the note.
        iii.   Cash interest is based on the face interest rate times the face value, while the effective interest is the market rate of interest times the carrying value of the note.

C. Sources of long-term debt financing.
1. Nonpublic sources of debt financing include individuals and institutions such as banks, savings and loans, and insurance companies.
   a. Collateral--used to protect creditors' claims.
      i. An asset or group of assets named in a debt agreement to which the creditor has claim if the borrower fails to comply with the terms of the note.
      ii. Mortgage--a long-term note that is secured with real estate.
   b. Leases--agreements to convey the use of a tangible asset from one party to another in return for rental payments.
      i. Operating lease--rental agreement for a period of time that is substantially shorter than the economic life of the leased asset.
      ii. Capital lease--for all practical purposes the user owns the asset.
2. Public sources of debt financing are known as bonds.
   a. Bonds are long-term debt instruments issued by corporations to raise money from the public.
      i. The amount of cash borrowed is based on the present value of the promised cash flows.
   b. Bond indenture--specifies the amount of the bond issue, the life of the bond, the face value of each bond, and the face interest rate on the bond issue.
   c. Bonds may have provisions.
      i. Registered bonds--numbered and made payable in the name of the bondholder.
      ii. Bearer bonds--made payable to the bearer or person who has physical possession of the bond.
      iii. Callable bonds--bonds that may be bought back at a specified price before the maturity date.
      iv. Convertible bonds--bondholders may exchange their bonds for common or preferred stock.
      v. Serial bonds--specified portions of the bonds come due periodically over the life of the bond issue.
      vi. Secured bonds--secured by assets of the issuing corporation.
      vii. Unsecured or debenture bonds--no specific assets are pledged as security.
      viii. Subordinate bonds--bonds whose rights to repayments are ranked after some other person or group of creditors.

III. Firms can examine the impact of financing alternatives by using pro forma financial statements.
   A. Compare results and ratios using the debt or equity financing alternatives.
      1. Debt-to-equity ratio.
      2. Times interest earned ratio.
      3. Return on assets.
      4. Return on equity.
   B. Selecting the appropriate debt instrument is part of the planning process.
      1. Forecast the cash inflows expected from the project being financed and then match them with an appropriate debt instrument.
         a. Compare the repayment schedules of the different debt financing alternatives.
         b. Cash flow is the most important factor when selecting the appropriate debt financing instrument.
   C. Financing budget--identifies how the firm has decided to finance long-term projects.

Problem I

Indicate whether the following statements are either true (T) or false (F).

_____1. Owners may use financial leverage to increase the rate of return on their investment.
_____2. Face value is the amount that must ultimately be repaid by the borrower.
_____3. The more stable a company's earnings, the greater the financial risk.
_____4. The interest portion of an installment payment becomes larger with each subsequent payment.
_____5. When the market rate of interest on a note is less than the face rate, a note will be issued at a premium.
_____6. Interest expense is the cost of using borrowed funds.
_____7. Any excess return generated from assets acquired using borrowed funds belongs to the creditors.
_____8. When the market rate equals the face rate, the cash proceeds will equal the face value of the note.
_____9. A periodic payment note will consist of equal amounts of interest and principal repayments over the life of the note.
_____10. A capital lease is typically for a period of time that is shorter than the economic life of the asset being leased.

Problem II

Indicate the correct answer by circling the appropriate letter.

<u>Use the following information for the next two questions</u>:

At the end of the current period, Roenick Corporation provided the following selected financial information:

Income before interest and taxes	$120,000
Total assets	950,000
Total liabilities	400,000
Total stockholders' equity	550,000
Interest expense	42,000
Income taxes	$ 35,000

1. Roenick's debt-to-equity ratio is _____.
    a. 0.727
    b. 1.375
    c. 0.300
    d. 0.421

2. Roenick's times interest earned is _____.
    a. 3.9
    b. 8.1
    c. 2.9
    d. 0.2

3. Which of the following will affect a company's financial risk?
    a. The company's debt-to-equity ratio.
    b. The volatility of a company's sales
    c. Both a and b are correct
    d. None of the above are correct

<u>Use the following information for the next two questions</u>:

Jinger Corporation borrowed $200,000 from a local bank. The loan is a periodic payment note with an interest rate of 10 percent. The annual payment is $32,509.

4. What is the interest portion of the first payment?
   a. $12,000
   b. $20,000
   c. $32,509
   d. $16,345

5. What is the loan balance after the first payment?
   a. $200,000
   b. $167,491
   c. $180,000
   d. $187,491

Use the following information for the next two questions:

On August 1, X Corporation issued a 10-year, $400,000 note payable with a face rate of interest of 9% payable annually. The market rate of interest was 12% and the cash proceeds of the note were $332,197.

6. What is the amount of the annual cash payment?
   a. $36,000
   b. $18,000
   c. $48,000
   d. $24,000

7. What is interest expense for the first period?
   a. $39,864
   b. $36,000
   c. $48,000
   d. $41,739

8. On January 1, X Corporation borrowed $100,000 agreeing to pay interest at a rate of 6%. Compute the periodic payment if the note is to repaid over the next 10 years.
   a. $13,587
   b. $10,000
   c. $8,931
   d. $12,794

9. On July 1, Z Corporation issued a 10-year, $200,000 note payable with a face rate of interest of 4%. Assuming a market rate of interest of 5% and annual payments, what will be the cash proceeds on the note?
   a. $200,000
   b. $191,784
   c. $167,352
   d. $184,554

10. On June 1, X Corporation issued a 5-year, $800,000 note payable with a face rate of interest of 8% payable semi-annually. The market rate of interest was 6%. What are the cash proceeds on the note?
    a. $756,984
    b. $812,539
    c. $868,242
    d. $891,006

Problem III

Following is a list of important ideas and key concepts from the chapter. To test your knowledge of these terms, match the term with the definition by placing the number in the space provided.

_____ bearer bond
_____ bond
_____ bond indenture
_____ callable bond
_____ capital lease
_____ carrying value of a note
_____ collateral
_____ convertible bond
_____ covenants
_____ debenture bonds

_____ financial leverage
_____ financial risk
_____ lease
_____ lump-sum payment note
_____ mortgage bond
_____ operating lease
_____ registered bonds
_____ secured bond
_____ serial bond
_____ unsecured bond

1. A bond that is secured with real estate

2. A bond feature that allows bondholders to exchange their bonds for common or preferred stock

3. A bond that has some part of the issuing corporation's assets serving as security for the loan

4. A rental agreement for a period of time substantially shorter than the economic life of the leased asset

5. A bond that does not have any specific assets pledged as security against its repayment

6. An asset or group of assets specifically named in a debt agreement to which the creditor has claim if the borrower fails to comply with the terms of the note

7. Bonds that are numbered and made payable in the name of the bondholder

8. A debt instrument that contains a promise to pay a specific amount of money at the end of a specified period of time

9. The bond contract

10. A lease in which a company acquires such a substantial interest in the leased property that the lessee company, for all practical purposes, owns the asset

11. The chance that a firm will default on its debt

12. An agreement to convey the use of a tangible asset from one party to another in return for rental payments

13. A long-term debt instrument issued by corporations to raise money from the public

14. A bond issue that has specified portions of the bond issue coming due periodically over the life of the bond issue

15. Restrictions that lenders place on the borrowing company to protect the lender's interest

16. A bond that is payable to the bearer or person who has physical possession of the bond

17. The face value of a note plus its remaining premium or minus its remaining discount

18. A bond that gives the firm issuing the bond the right to buy it back before the maturity date at a specified price

19. A financing strategy designed to increase the rate of return on owners' investment by generating a greater return on borrowed funds than the cost of using the funds

20. Unsecured bonds; bonds with no specific assets pledged as collateral

Problem IV

Complete the following sentences by filling in the correct response.

1. The risk of debt financing is called _____ risk.

2. The _____ of a note refers to the cash received by the borrower whereas the _____ _____ refers to the amount the borrower must repay.

3. When the market rate of interest is _____ than the face rate of interest, the proceeds of the note will be less than the face value of the note.

4. The contract that specifies the terms and conditions related to a bond is called the _____ _____.

5. A _____ bond is secured by a company's real estate whereas a _____ bond is unsecured.

6. The larger the debt-to-equity ratio, the greater the amount of _____ used to finance the company's operations, and the greater the _____ risk.

7. Firms use _____ liabilities to finance assets such as buildings, equipment, land and patents.

Problem V

Y Corporation issued a five-year, $50,000 face value, noninterest-bearing note payable on January 1, 19X1. The effective rate of interest on the note was 8% compounded semiannually.

a. What amount will Y Corporation receive on January 1, 19X1?

b. What amount will Y Corporation repay on the maturity date?

c. What amount of interest will be incurred by the borrower for 19X1?

Problem VI

On September 1, 1999, Lintner Company borrowed $300,000 from the bank. Under the terms of the loan, Lintner will make five annual payments of interest and principal. The interest rate on the note is 8 percent. Prepare an amortization schedule for the periodic note payable (see Exhibit 18.3).

Problem VII

Vectar Corporation issued a $2,000,000, 20-year bond payable on March 1, 1999. The bond carries a face rate of 9 percent payable annually. The market rate was 7 percent on the date the bond was issued and the cash proceeds of the bond were $2,423,760.57. Prepare the bond amortization schedule for the first three years of the bond (see Exhibit 18.8).

Pause and Reflect

Why might the effective interest rate not equal the face rate of interest printed on a note payable?

Solutions for Chapter 18

Problem I

1. T
2. T
3. F
4. F
5. T
6. T
7. F
8. T
9. F
10. F

Problem II

1. a
2. c
3. c
4. b
5. d
6. a
7. a
8. a
9. d
10. c

Problem III

16 bearer bond
13 bond
9 bond indenture
18 callable bond
10 capital lease
17 carrying value of a note
6 collateral
2 convertible bond
15 covenants
20 debenture bonds

19 financial leverage
11 financial risk
12 lease
8 lump-sum payment note
1 mortgage bond
4 operating lease
7 registered bonds
3 secured bond
14 serial bond
5 unsecured bond

Problem IV

1. financial
2. proceeds, face value
3. greater
4. bond indenture
5. mortgage, debenture
6. debt, financial
7. long-term

Problem V

a. $50,000 \times PV(4\%, 10)$ = cash proceeds

      $50,000 \times .6756 = \$33,780$

b.   The face value of the note ($50,000) must be repaid at maturity.

c.   Interest for first 6 months:

      $\$33,780 \times .08 \times 6/12 = \$1,351.20$

    Interest for last 6 months:

      ($33780 + $1,351.20) $\times .08 \times 6/12 = \$35,131.20 \times .08 \times 6/12 = \$1,405.25$

    Total interest expense for the year:

      $\$1,351.20 + \$1,405.25 = \$2,756.45$

Problem VI

Periodic Payment   Annuity X PVA(5,8%) = $300,000
                             Annuity X 3.9927 = $300,000
                             Annuity = $75,137.13

Date	(a) Payment	(b) Interest Expense [.08 x (d)]	(c) Principal [(a) - (b)]	(d) Loan Balance [(d) - (c)]
9/1/99				$300,000.00
9/1/00	$75,137.13	$24,000.00	$51,137.13	$248,862.87
9/1/01	$75,137.13	$19,909.03	$55,228.10	$193,634.77
9/1/02	$75,137.13	$15,490.78	$59,646.35	$133,988.42
9/1/03	$75,137.13	$10,719.07	$64,418.06	$ 69,570.36
9/1/04	$75,137.13	$ 5,566.77*	$69,570.36	$ - 0 -

* rounding

Problem VII

Date	(a) Cash Interest [.09 x $2,000,000]	(b) Interest Expense [.07 x (e)]	(c) Amortized Premium [(a) - (b)]	(d) Remaining Premium [(d) - (c)]	(e) Carrying Value [(e) - (c)]
3/1/99				$423,760.57	$2,423,760.57
31/00	$180,000.00	$169,663.24	$10,336.76	$413,423.81	$2,413,423.81
3/1/01	$180,000.00	$168,939.67	$11,060.33	$402,363.48	$2,402,363.48
3/1/02	$180,000.00	$168,165.44	$11,834.56	$390,528.92	$2,390,528.92

Pause and Reflect

There are several possible reasons for an effective rate of interest differing from the amount shown on the note. Economic conditions may have changed, such as a change in the prime lending rate, resulting in changes in the market rate of interest. The creditor may also perceive that the issuer of the note has a higher or lower level of business risk. For example, if the issuer of the note has been experiencing sluggish or declining sales, the creditor may require a greater rate of return than printed on the note.

Chapter 19
Recording and Communicating Equity Financing Activities

Chapter Overview

In Chapter 17, planning equity financing activities was presented. This chapter extends that discussion by examining the process for recording and communicating these activities through the accounting system during the performance phase. The chapter will illustrate the process for recording contributions by owners, distributions to owners, and other equity-financing issues for sole proprietorships, partnerships, and corporations. Simple capital accounts are used to show the owners' interest for sole proprietorships and partnerships because the organizations are not separate legal entities. Because corporations are separate legal entities and their owners have limited liability, the stockholders' equity is reported in two sections: contributed capital and retained earnings.

As you study this chapter, it may be necessary to review the terms and concepts presented in Chapter 17. Make sure you understand the equity-financing events; don't try to memorize all the journal entries associated with these accounting events. You'll only become confused. Distinguish clearly in your mind the differences in accounting for equity financing activities of sole proprietorships, partnerships, and corporations.

Read and Recall Questions

> **Learning Objective:**
> L.O.1. Describe how to record and communicate equity financing activities for sole proprietorships and partnerships.

Why do sole proprietorships use only one account to summarize the owner's contribution and interest in the firm's undistributed earnings?

If a sole proprietorship has a net income of $7,300, what entry would be recorded to represent the change in owner's equity?

What is a drawing account? What account classification does it have?

Are withdrawals by the proprietor an expense of the business? Explain.

What is the purpose of the statement of changes in owner's equity?

How many capital and drawing accounts will a partnership have?

When partners contribute assets other than cash, at what value will the assets be recorded?

What is the form of the entry used to record the allocation of a loss generated by a partnership assuming there are three partners, A, B, and C?

What is the purpose of the statement of changes in partners' capital?

If an existing partner sells all or part of his or interest in the firm directly to a new partner, what is the impact on the total partnership equity?

If a new partner invests an amount greater than the ownership interest credited to his or her capital account, how is the bonus to the existing partners divided?

If a new partner receives an ownership interest in the partnership greater than the amount invested, what happens to the existing partners' capital accounts?

When a partner withdraws from the partnership and receives less than the amount of his or her ownership interest, what happens to the remaining partners' capital accounts?

Learning Objective:
L.O.2. Explain how and why corporations record contributed capital.

Why does corporate accounting separate the contributions made by stockholders from the undistributed earnings of the firm?

If stock has a par value, what amount is always credited to the capital stock account?

What does the account Paid-in Capital in Excess of Par represent? When is it used?

If no-par stock is issued, what amount appears in the capital stock account? If no-par stated value stock is issued, what amount appears in the capital stock account?

If stock is issued for assets other than cash, at what amount will the transaction be recorded?

What is donated capital? Why would a corporation have donated capital?

Learning Objective:
L.O.3. Demonstrate how corporate earnings and losses are determined and how a firm's earnings are distributed to its owners.

What is retained earnings? What is the normal account balance for the account Retained Earnings?

What does a deficit in retained earnings mean?

How does a net income change retained earnings? A net loss?

What effect does the declaration of dividends have on retained earnings? What effect does the entry on the date of dividend distribution have on retained earnings?

What is a small stock dividend? What value is used to record a small stock dividend?

What type of account is Stock Dividends Distributable?

What is a large stock dividend? What value is used to record a large stock dividend?

Learning Objective:
L.O.4. Explain why corporations buy treasury stock and/or split their stock and how to account for these events.

What is treasury stock? What type of account is Treasury Stock? What is its normal balance?

When is the Paid-in Capital from Treasury Stock Transactions account used? Would this account ever be debited? Explain.

Would the Retained Earnings account ever be debited when reissuing treasury stock? Explain.

Why is no entry recorded for a stock split?

Learning Objective:
L.O.5. Describe the format of a corporation's stockholders' equity and explain why the format is used.

What is the purpose of the statement of retained earnings?

Stockholders' equity is divided into two categories: contributed capital and retained earnings. What does contributed capital represent? Retained earnings?

What effect does treasury stock have on contributed capital?

Excluding net income, where are equity events reported on the cash flows statement?

Outline of Key Concepts

I. Sole proprietorships and partnerships have economic but not legal distinctions from the owners.
   A. Sole proprietorship requires only one permanent balance sheet equity account, the owner's capital account.
      1. The capital account's balance changes at the end of an accounting period as revenue and expense accounts are closed to Income Summary, and the resulting net income is in turn closed to the capital account.
      2. When an owner withdraws assets from the business for personal use, the amount is usually recorded in a separate drawing account.
         a. The drawing account is a contra equity account and is closed to the capital account at the end of the accounting period.
         b. Withdrawals are not expenses of the business but are distributions of the earnings or investment to the owner.
      3. After closing entries, the capital account balance reflects all owner contributions to the firm plus accumulated net income less withdrawals.
   B. Accounting for partnership equity requires a separate capital and drawing account for each partner in order to determine each owner's interest in the firm.
      1. Assets other than cash are recorded at their fair market value at the time of contribution.
      2. The income or loss generated by the partnership during the period is allocated to the partners, resulting in an increase or decrease to the respective capital accounts.
         a. See Chapter 17 for commonly used methods for dividing earnings.

3. Admitting a new partner dissolves the old partnership and creates a new partnership.
   a. New partner may purchase all or part of the interest of an existing partner by payment to the existing partner.
      i. New partner receives all or a portion of the selling partner's capital.
      ii. This transaction does not change the amount of the assets of the firm.
   b. New partner may invest directly in the partnership organization.
      i. The payment of cash or other assets increases the amount of the firm's total assets as well as its total owners' equity.
      ii. New partner's interest in the firm is either the same, smaller, or larger than the amount of the assets contributed.
      iii. If a new partner is required to pay a price greater than the amount credited to his or her capital account, the excess is viewed as a bonus to the existing partners.
      iv. If a new partner receives a capital credit greater than the price paid, the excess capital credit is a bonus to the new partner.
   c. Partnership may revalue its assets before admitting a new partner if the partnership structure has not changed for an extended period of time or when asset values have changed substantially.
4. A partner's withdrawal may occur in one of three ways.
   a. His or her interest may be purchased by one or more of the remaining partners.
      i. On the partnership books, this involves an exchange of capital only.
   b. His or her interest may be purchased by an outsider seeking admission to the partnership.
      i. For the partnership, this involves an exchange of capital only.
   c. His or her interest may be purchased by the partnership itself.
      i. The amount paid may equal, exceed, or be less than the balance in the withdrawing partner's capital account.

II. Accounting for corporate owners' equity makes a distinction between the contributions made by stockholders and the reinvested earnings of the firm.
   A. Cash and other resources given by stockholders and others to the corporation are classified as contributed capital.
      1. When accounting for par value stock, the par value is credited to the capital stock account regardless of the amount paid for the shares.
         a. The excess amount is recorded in a Paid-in Capital in Excess of Par account.
      2. When accounting for no-par stock, the amount received for the shares is credited to the capital stock account.
      3. When accounting for no-par stated value stock, the stated value of the stock is credited to the capital stock account.
         a. The excess amount is recorded in a Paid-in Capital in Excess of Stated Value account.

4. When the transaction does not involve cash, the fair market value of the stock issued or of the goods or services received, whichever is more readily determined, provides the cash equivalent amount.
5. Donated capital reflects the dollar value of the assets contributed to a corporation.
   a. No shares of stock are issued in return.

B. The accumulation and distribution of corporate earnings is accounted for separately from contributions by owners.
   1. Retained earnings reports the amount of a corporation's earnings since its inception less all dividends distributed.
      a. The account has a normal credit balance that represents the amount of earnings reinvested in the corporation.
      b. A debit balance is referred to as a deficit in retained earnings.
   2. Net income increases a firm's net assets and the stockholders' interest in the firm as a result of ongoing activities.
      a. Revenues and expenses are closed to Income Summary.
      b. The balance of Income Summary (which represents net income or loss) is then closed to Retained Earnings.
   3. When dividends are declared, the corporation incurs and records a liability in the amount of the dividends declared.
      a. The dividend is also typically recorded in a temporary account called Dividend Declared.
      b. The Dividends Declared account is then closed to Retained Earnings at the end of the accounting period.
   4. Stock dividends may be issued to stockholders so that cash may be retained in the business.
      a. Small stock dividends.
         i. The additional number of shares to be issued is small, usually 20 to 25 percent or less of the shares outstanding.
         ii. Debit Retained Earnings for the fair market value of the shares to be issued.
         iii. Stock Dividends Distributable is credited for the par value of the stock.
         iv. Any excess of the market value over the par value is credited to the Paid-in Capital in Excess of Par account.
      b. Large stock dividends.
         i. The number of additional shares is greater than 25 percent of the shares outstanding.
         ii. The transaction is recorded at the par value rather than the market value of the stock.

C. Accounting for additional corporate equity events.
   1. Treasury stock is a company's own stock reacquired with the intent of reissuing at a later date.
      a. It is not an asset of the corporation; it is a contra equity account that reduces total stockholders' equity on the balance sheet.

  b. The treasury shares are still considered to be issued but not outstanding.
  c. The purchase price of treasury shares is recorded as a debit to Treasury Stock.
  d. If treasury stock is reissued at an amount in excess of the purchase price, the excess is recorded in a contributed capital account called Paid-in Capital from Treasury Stock Transactions.
  e. If the treasury stock is reissued at an amount less than the purchase price, the difference is debited to the Paid-in Capital from Treasury Stock Transactions account.
   i. If the paid-in capital account balance is not sufficient, Retained Earnings is debited.
 2. A stock split occurs when a corporation calls in all the shares issued, reducing the par value of the shares, and issues a larger number of new shares in their place.
  a. It does not change the balance in any stockholders' equity accounts.
  b. It simply reduces the par value of the stock and increases the number of shares authorized, issued, and outstanding.

III. Reporting corporate equity events.
 A. Statement of retained earnings.
  1. Shows the effects of operating performance and dividend policy on the stockholders' interest in the corporation.
  2. Ending balance is reported in the stockholders' equity section of the balance sheet.
 B. Balance sheet--stockholders' equity section reports both contributed capital and retained earnings.
  1. Contributed capital section--reports the dollar amount of resources contributed to the corporation from the stockholders and others.
  2. Retained earnings--reflects the earnings reinvested in the corporation.
  3. Treasury stock reduces the sum of the contributed capital and retained earnings.
 C. Cash flows statement.
  1. Cash from net income is reported in the operating section of the statement.
  2. All other equity events are reported in the financing section of the statement.

Problem I

Indicate whether the following statements are either true (T) or false (F).

_____ 1. The par value of a share of stock is the minimum issue price allowed by law.
_____ 2. Withdrawals by partners will be considered expenses of the partnership.
_____ 3. A credit balance in retained earnings would be considered a deficit in retained earnings.
_____ 4. In a sole proprietorship, net income is closed to the owner's capital account.
_____ 5. Stock dividends cause a corporation's net assets to decrease.
_____ 6. The drawing account is considered a contra equity account.
_____ 7. On the formation of a partnership, assets will be recorded at their original cost to the incoming partner.
_____ 8. A corporation is not considered a separate legal entity.
_____ 9. Once a dividend has been declared, a liability for payment exists for the corporation.
_____ 10. Dividends are not paid on treasury stock.
_____ 11. For corporations, contributions made by stockholders are separated from reinvested earnings.
_____ 12. If common stock is sold for more than its par value, the corporation will recognize a gain.
_____ 13. A "small" stock dividend will be recorded at the stock's fair market value.
_____ 14. Treasury stock is considered an asset of the corporation.

Problem II

Indicate the correct answer by circling the appropriate letter.

1. Andy Jones started a sole proprietorship on January 1, 19X1 by contributing $50,000 in assets. During the first year of operations, the company reported net income of $22,000 and Andy withdrew $6,000 from the business for personal use. The balance in the Jones, Capital account at the end of the year will be _____.
   a. $50,000
   b. $72,000
   c. $66,000
   d. $78,000

2. On September 13, Jack Jones withdrew $12,000 from the JJ Partnership. The partnership entry to record the withdrawal will be _____.

    a.   Cash $12,000
            Jones, Drawing $12,000
    b.   Jones, Capital $12,000
            Cash $12,000
    c.   Income Summary $12,000
            Cash $12,000
    d.   Jones, Drawing $12,000
            Cash $12,000

3. Max and Mary formed the M&M Partnership on January 1, 19X1 by each contributing $50,000 cash. Since Mary will manage daily operations, she is to receive a salary allocation of $35,000 each year. Any remaining profits or losses will be shared equally. M&M reported net income of $25,000 for 9X1. Mary's capital account balance at the end of the year will be _____.

    a. $50,000
    b. $85,000
    c. $62,500
    d. $80,000

4. When partners contribute assets to the partnership, the assets will be recorded at _____.

    a. the assets fair market value at the time it is contributed
    b. the original cost of the asset to the partner
    c. the undepreciated cost of the asset to the partner
    d. none of the above are correct

5. X Corporation issued 200,000 shares of its $20 par value common stock. The issue price was $30 per share. The journal entry made by X Corporation on the issue date would be _____.

    a.   Cash   6,000,000
            Common Stock   4,000,000
            Paid-in Capital in Excess of Par - Common Stock   2,000,000
    b.   Cash   6,000,000
            Common Stock   6,000,000
    c.   Cash   6,000,000
            Common Stock   4,000,000
            Gain on sale of Common Stock   2,000,000
    d. none of the above

6. On July 1, Y Corporation declared a 30 percent stock dividend. On the date declared, there were 10,000 shares of $20 par value common stock outstanding. The fair market value per share prior to the declaration of the dividend was $35. The entry on July 1 will include _____.
    a. a debit to cash of $60,000
    b. a debit to cash of $105,000
    c. a credit to stock dividends distributable of $105,000
    d. a credit to stock dividends distributable of $60,000

7. On January 16, Z Corporation declared a 5 percent stock dividend. On the date declared, there were 20,000 shares of $10 par value common stock outstanding. The fair market value per share prior to the declaration of the dividend was $17. The entry on January 16 to record the declaration of the stock dividend is _____.

    a. Retained earnings $17,000
           Stock dividend distributable $10,000
           Paid-in-capital, common stock $ 7,000
    b. Stock dividend distributable $10,000
         Paid-in-capital, common stock $ 7,000
           Retained earnings $17,000
    c. Retained earnings $10,000
           Common stock $10,000
    d. Retained earnings $17,000
           Common stock $10,000
           Paid-in-capital, common stock $ 7,000

8. On January 1, Jerry Minter sold his partnership interest to Mary King for $30,000. Minter's capital account balance was $19,000 at the time of the sale. The partnership entry to record the change in partnership ownership is _____.

    a. Cash $30,000
           King, capital $30,000
    b. Cash $30,000
           Minter, capital $19,000
           Gain on sale $11,000
    c. Minter, capital $19,000
           King, capital $19,000
    d. Minter, capital $19,000
         Loss on sale $11,000
           King, capital $30,000

9. During the year, Fasttax Corporation reported net income of $235,000 and paid cash dividends of $85,000. The beginning balance in retained earnings was $400,000. What will Fasttax report as retained earnings on the balance sheet as of the end of the year?
   a. $400,000
   b. $635,000
   c. $165,000
   d. $550,000

10. A cash dividend will reduce retained earnings on the _____.
    a. declaration date
    b. ex-dividend date
    c. date of record
    d. date of distribution

11. Which of the following will not reduce total stockholders' equity?
    a. The purchase of treasury stock.
    b. The company reported a net loss for the year.
    c. The company paid a cash dividend.
    d. The company issued a stock dividend.

12. A cash dividend will be shown in the _____ section of the cash flow statement.
    a. cash flows from operations
    b. cash flows from financing activities
    c. cash flows from investing activities
    d. non-cash activities

13. The purchase of treasury stock will be shown in the _____ section of the cash flow statement.
    a. cash flows from operations
    b. cash flows from financing activities
    c. cash flows from investing activities
    d. non-cash activities

©The McGraw-Hill Companies, Inc., 2000

Problem III

Following is a list of important ideas and key concepts from the chapter. To test your knowledge of these terms, match the term with the definition by placing the number in the space provided.

_____ deficit in retained earnings
_____ donated capital
_____ drawing account
_____ statement of changes in partners' capital
_____ stock dividends distributable

1. An account that reflects the dollar value of the assets given to a corporation that increases the contributed capital of the corporation's stockholders' equity but does not change the number of shares or shareholders

2. An account credited on the date of declaration of a stock dividend to show the par value of the shares the corporation will issue on the date of payment

3. A negative or debit balance in the Retained Earnings account created when the cumulative total of net losses plus dividends declared exceeds the cumulative total of net income

4. A financial statement that presents the changes in the individual partners' capital balances that result from additional contributions, the firm's income or loss, and the partners' withdrawals from the firm over a specific period of time

5. A contra equity account used in proprietorship and partnership accounting to summarize the dollar amount of assets withdrawn from the business entity for personal use

Problem IV

1. In a corporation, _____ made by stockholders are kept separate from undistributed _____ of the firm.

2. The amount of _____ value is credited to the capital stock account regardless of the amount _____ for the shares.

3. The _____ capital account reflects assets given to a corporation. As a result, contributed capital of the corporation's stockholders' equity _____, but the number of _____ is not affected.

4. _____ _____ is the amount of corporate earnings since inception that has not been _____ to shareholders as _____.

5. A stock split will change the _____ _____ of the stock and will cause the number of shares outstanding to _____.

Problem V

Bob and Carol, partners in the Canter Partnership, wish to admit Bill into the partnership. At the time of admission, Bob and Carol had the following capital account balances:

    Bob, Capital $300,000
    Carol, Capital $200,000

Required: Prepare the necessary journal entry under each admission assumption.

a. Bill will purchase one-half of Carol's interest for $140,000.

b. Bill will contribute $100,000 to the partnership for a 15 percent interest in the partnership. Any bonus will be credited to the existing partners in relation to their preadmittance capital account balances.

c. Bill will contibute $60,000 for a 15 percent interest in the partnership. Any bonus will be credited to Bill and will be borne by Bob and Carol in relation to their preadmittance capital account balances.

Problem VI.

Events affecting the stockholders' equity section of the Solex Corporation are presented below. On the general journal provided on the following page, prepare all necessary journal entries for the year.

1/11   One thousand shares of no-par, no-stated value common stock were issued for $7 per share.

3/29   Land was purchased by the company by issuing 20,000 shares of no-par, no-stated value common stock. The market price per share was $8.

6/30   The board of directors declared a cash dividend of $1 per share. There were 100,000 shares outstanding on the date of declaration. The date of record is 7/5 and payment date is 7/9.

7/9   Solex paid the cash dividend declared on 6/30.

8/3   Solex repurchased 1,000 shares of its own stock for $7.50 per share.

10/15   The board of directors declared a 5 percent stock dividend to be issued on 10/25. On the date of declaration, there were 99,000 shares outstanding. The market price per share was $8.25.

10/25   The stock certificates related to the stock dividend on 10/15 were distributed.

12/12   The stock repurchased by Solex on 8/3 was resold for $9.50 per share.

Problem VI (continued)

General Journal

Date	Account Title	Debit	Credit

Pause and Reflect

Treasury stock is a company's own stock reacquired with the intent of reissuing it at a later date. If a company declares a 20% stock dividend, would the treasury shares receive the stock dividend? Why or why not?

_____
_____
_____
_____
_____

Solutions for Chapter 19

Problem I

1. T
2. F
3. F
4. T
5. F
6. T
7. F
8. F
9. T
10. T
11. T
12. F
13. T
14. F

Problem II

1. c
2. d
3. d
4. a
5. a
6. d
7. a
8. c
9. d
10. a
11. d
12. b
13. b

Problem III

3   deficit in retained earnings
1   donated capital
5   drawing account

4   statement of changes in partners' capital
2   stock dividends distributable

Problem IV

1. contributions, earnings
2. par, paid
3. donated, increases, shares
4. Retained earnings, distributed, dividends
5. par value, increase

Problem V

a.   Carol, Capital $100,000
        Bill, Capital $100,000

b.   Cash $100,000
        Bob, Capital $ 6,000
        Carol, Capital $ 4,000
        Bill, Capital $90,000

Credit to Bill's capital account = ($100,000 + $500,000) X .15 = $90,000

Allocation of bonus to existing partners:
    Bob = $300,000/$500,000 X ($100,000 - $90,000) = $6,000
    Carol = $200,000/$500,000 X ($100,000 - $90,000) = $4,000

c.   Cash $60,000
        Bob, Capital $14,400
        Carol, Capital $ 9,600
        Bill, Capital $84,000

Credit to Bill's capital account = ($60,000 + $500,000) X .15 = $84,000

Allocation of bonus to existing partners:
    Bob = $300,000/$500,000 X ($60,000 - $84,000) = <$14,400>
    Carol = $200,000/$500,000 X ($60,000 - $84,000) = <$9,600>

Problem VI

General Journal

Date	Account Title	Debit	Credit
1/11	Cash	7,000	
	Common Stock		7,000
3/29	Land	160,000	
	Common Stock		160,000
6/30	Dividends	100,000	
	Dividends Payable		100,000
7/9	Dividends Payable	100,000	
	Cash		100,000
8/3	Treasury Stock	7,500	
	Cash		7,500
10/15	Retained Earnings	40,838	
	Stock Dividends Distributable		40,838
	(99,000 X .05 X $8.25)		
10/25	Stock Dividends Distributable	40,838	
	Common Stock		40,838
12/12	Cash	9,500	
	Treasury Stock		7,500
	Paid-in Capital - Treasury Stock		2,000

Pause and Reflect

No, the treasury shares would not receive additional shares as a result of the stock dividend. Stock dividends are only issued on outstanding stock or stock that is in the hands of stockholders. A corporation does not own itself when it holds treasury stock. Treasury stock is a temporary reduction in owners' equity, so treasury shares are not considered to be outstanding shares of stock. Therefore, no stock dividends are declared on treasury stock.

Chapter 20
Recording and Communicating Long-Term Debt Financing Activities

Chapter Overview

Chapter 20 illustrates the process for recording and communicating debt-financing activities. Each of the three types of notes (periodic payment, lump-sum payment, and periodic and lump-sum payment) receives a slightly different accounting treatment. The cash flows specified by the notes differ according to the type of note and the market interest rate promised by the notes. The accounting records will reflect the long-term obligation created by the notes as well as the cost of using long-term debt financing. The chapter demonstrates the accounting for premiums and discounts on bonds, and it presents the accounting for early retirement of debt.

As you study this chapter, you will want to refer to Chapter 18 on planning debt financing. Many of the terms introduced in that chapter will be referenced in Chapter 20. You will also apply the time value of money concepts learned in Chapter 14. Seek to understand the cash flow effects of each of the types of notes. As you learn how to prepare amortization tables, notice the effect that the amortization of bond premiums and discounts has on the interest cost of using debt financing. This chapter will require focused study time and practice working problems and excercises.

Read and Recall Questions

> **Learning Objective:**
> L.O.1. Explain how and why companies record and communicate activities concerning long-term periodic payment notes.

Distinguish among periodic payment, lump-sum payment, and periodic payment and lump-sum payment notes.

Does the total amount of each payment of an installment note represent a reduction in the principal of the note? Explain.

How is the principal of an installment note reported on the balance sheet?

How is the payment on an installment note reported on the cash flows statement?

Learning Objective:
L.O.2. Describe how and why companies record and communicate events pertaining to long-term lump-sum (noninterest-bearing) notes.

What determines the face value of a lump-sum payment note?

What does the account Discount on Note Payable represent? What type of account is Discount on Note Payable?

As the Discount on Note Payable account is reduced, what happens to the carrying value of the note payable?

When do the cash flows associated with a lump-sum payment note occur?

Learning Objective:
L.O.3. Illustrate how and why companies record and communicate bond financing.

What are bonds?

If the market rate equals the face rate of interest, are the proceeds of the bond issue equal to, greater than, or less than the face value of the bonds? Explain.

If the market rate equals the face rate of interest, is the interest expense equal to, greater than, or less than the cash interest paid? Explain.

When will bonds be reclassified from a long-term liability to a current liability?

If the market rate is greater than the face rate of interest, will the proceeds be equal to, greater than, or less than the face value of the bonds? Explain.

If the market rate is greater than the face rate of interest, will the interest expense be equal to, greater than, or less than the cash interest paid? Explain.

What is the purpose of a bond amortization table?

What does the account Discount on Bonds Payable represent? Why type of account is Discount on Bonds Payable?

How is the carrying value of bonds issued at a discount reported on the balance sheet?

If the market rate is less than the face rate of interest, will the proceeds be equal to, greater than, or less than the face amount of the bonds? Explain.

If the market rate is less than the face rate of interest, will interest expense be equal to, greater than, or less than the cash interest paid? Explain.

What does the account Premium on Bonds Payable represent? What type of account is Premium on Bonds Payable?

How is the carrying value of a bond issued at a premium reported on the balance sheet?

What are the three ways that are usually used for the early retirement of bonds?

Why would companies want to retire bonds early?

Does a company recognize a gain or loss, when the purchase price exceeds the bonds' carrying value?

Explain the call feature of a bond issue.

If bonds are convertible, with whom does the decision to convert bonds to stock rest?

Learning Objective:
L.O.4. Explain how and why companies record and communicate operating and capital leases.

Distinguish between operating and capital leases.

What account is debited for each payment of an operating lease?

When a lessee signs a capital lease, what type of account is debited and what type of account is credited?

At what amount is the capital lease obligation recorded? At what amount is the asset recorded?

Under a capital lease, the lease liability takes the form of an installment note. Explain why this is the case.

Why would some companies want to avoid capital leases?

141

Why are external decision-makers interested in information about a firm's long-term debt?

How do internal decision-makers use information about a firm's long-term debt?

Outline of Key Concepts

I. Accounting for long-term notes payable varies with the type of note.
   A. Accounting for periodic payment long-term notes (installment notes) requires timely recognition of the interest expense on the notes.
      1. The note is recorded at the present value of the annuity payments.
      2. A repayment schedule shows the portion of each payment that covers the interest on the loan and the portion that reduces the principal of the note.
         a. Journal entries mirror the repayment schedule.
      3. Interest expense will be reported on the income statement.
      4. Interest payments will be recorded in the operating section of the cash flows statement.
      5. Payments applied to the principal will be reported in the financing section of the cash flows statement.
      6. The notes and interest payable will be reported as liabilities on the balance sheet.
         a. The portion of the note due in the coming year is classified as a current liability.
   B. Lump-sum payment long-term notes payable (noninterest-bearing) do not have a face interest rate on the note.
      1. In accounting for these notes, it is important to use the appropriate market rate of interest to value the notes.
      2. The market rate is used to calculate the present value of the note payable.
      3. The note is recorded at the face amount of the note and a discount account is utilized to offset or reduce the liability so that it reflects the carrying value of the note.

    a. Entries to reflect interest show a credit to Discount on Notes Payable and a debit to Interest Expense.
    b. As the discount account is reduced, the carrying value of the note payable increases.
    c. At maturity, the carrying value of the note will equal the face amount of the note.
  C. Accounting for bonds (periodic payment and lump-sum long-term notes payable) is dependent upon the face rate and market rate of interest at the time the bonds are issued.
    1. If the market rate and face rate of interest are equal at the time the bonds are issued, the proceeds of the sale of the bonds equal the face value of the bonds.
      a. Interest expense equals the amount of cash interest paid.
    2. If the market rate of interest is greater than the face rate of the bond issue, the proceeds from the sale of the bonds are less than the face value of the bonds.
      a. The resulting discount is amortized over the life of the bonds.
      b. Discount on Bonds Payable is a contra liability account and is subtracted from Bonds Payable to show the bonds' carrying value.
      c. The amortization of the discount results in a higher amount of interest expense being reported on the income statement than cash interest being reported on the cash flows statement.
      d. At the maturity date, the discount will be fully amortized so that the carrying value of the bonds equals the face value of the bonds.
    3. If the market rate of interest is less than the face rate of interest of the bond issue, the proceeds from the sale of the bonds are greater than the face value of the bonds.
      a. The resulting premium is amortized over the life of the bonds.
      b. The balance in Premium on Bonds Payable is added to Bonds Payable to determine the carrying value of the bonds.
      c. The premium represents a reduction in interest expense.
        i. Amortization of the premium results in a lesser amount of interest expense being reported on the income statement than the cash interest reported on the cash flows statement.
      d. At the maturity date, the premium will be fully amortized so that the carrying value of the bonds equals the face value of the bonds.
  D. Early retirement of bonds usually occurs in one of three ways.
    1. A company can retire bonds by buying its bonds in the secondary bond market where the bonds are traded among investors.
      a. This becomes attractive when interest rates increase and the bond prices decrease.
      b. When the purchase price exceeds the bonds' carrying value, the company recognizes a loss.
      c. If the purchase price is less than the carrying value, the company recognizes a gain.

2. Bonds may be retired when a company calls the bonds or pays off the debt before their maturity date.
   a. The bonds' call feature specifies the call price and conditions under which the bonds may be paid early.
3. Bonds may be retired early if bondholders convert their bonds into stock.
   a. The decision to convert bonds rests with bondholders and not with the corporation.
   b. Bondholders will convert their bonds into stock only when the value of the stock they will receive exceeds the value of the bonds.

II. Accounting for operating leases and capital leases differs.
   A. Operating leases are essentially rental agreements.
      1. Payments may the lessee to the lessor for the use of an asset is considered rent expense.
   B. Capital leases confer such a substantial interest in the leased asset to the lessee that, in economic substance, the lessee owns the asset.
      1. Lessee records an asset for the leased property and a related liability for the lease obligation.
         a. The lease obligation is equal to the present value of the future lease payments.
         b. The asset is recorded at the sum of the present value of the lease payments plus any cash payments made at the time the lease is signed.
      2. Subsequent entries for lease payments are like those made for installment notes.

III. Decision-makers use information about debt financing in a variety of ways.
   A. External decision-makers want to know the amount, type, and cost of a firm's long-term debt, as well as its related cash flows.
      1. Used to assess the risk and rewards associated with debt financing.
      2. Provides a basis for deciding among investment alternatives.
   B. Internal decision-makers use information about debt-financing to balance the risk and reward of using funds obtained through long-term debt.
      1. Use to select the financing alternative with the smallest cost possible.
      2. Identify potential problems in meeting the cash flow obligations required by the firm's long-term debt.

Problem I

Indicate whether the following statements are either true (T) or false (F).

_____ 1. A periodic payment note is recorded at the present value of the annuity payments.
_____ 2. Interest payments will be shown in the financing section of the cash flow statement.
_____ 3. The market rate of interest is used to calculate the present value of a note payable.
_____ 4. Repayment of the principal portion of a note payable will be shown in the financing section of the cash flow statement.
_____ 5. The carrying value of a lump-sum note payable will get larger each time the company records interest expense.
_____ 6. Discount on bonds payable is a contra liability account.
_____ 7. If the repurchase price of a bond is less than its carrying value, then the company will recognize a loss on early retirement of bonds.
_____ 8. At maturity, the carrying value of a note is equal to its face value.
_____ 9. The decision to convert bonds into stock rests with the company and not the bondholder.
_____ 10. Capital leases have the economic substance of a purchase by using an installment note payable.

Problem II

Indicate the correct answer by circling the appropriate letter.

1. On December 1, 19X1 Z Corporation purchased equipment by issuing a 5-year $400,000 non-interest bearing note payable. The market rate of interest was 8 percent. The entry to record the purchase of the equipment will include a _____.
   a. debit to the equipment account of $400,000
   b. debit to the equipment account of $272,240
   c. debit to notes payable of $400,000
   d. credit to notes payable of $272,240

Use the following information for the next three questions:

On January 1, 19X1, Y Corporation purchased $100,000 of equipment by issuing an installment note payable. The note payable pays interest of 12 percent and is to be repaid in equal installments over the next ten years. Payments will be made each December 31.

2. What is the periodic payment that Y Corporation must make to repay the $100,000 loan?
   a. $17,698
   b. $15,690
   c. $21,335
   d. $17,211

3. What amount of interest expense will Y Corporation report in 19X1?
   a. $9,000
   b. $8,456
   c. $12,000
   d. $11,700

4. What will Y Corporation report as a liability on its balance sheet on December 31, 19X1?
   a. $100,000
   b. $98,000
   c. $93,140
   d. $94,302

5. On an installment note payable, interest expense will _____.
   a. become larger each year
   b. become smaller each year
   c. remain the same throughout the life of the note payable
   d. none of the above

Use the following information for the next two questions:

Box Inc. issued 20-year bonds with a $3,000,000 face value and a 6 percent face rate. At the time of the issue, the market rate of interest was 8 percent. Interest is paid annually.

6. What is the annual cash payment made by Box Inc.?
   a. $180,000
   b. $240,000
   c. $300,000
   d. $200,000

7. Which of the following entries would have been made on the issue date of the bond?

    a.   Cash   3,000,000

            Bonds Payable   3,000,000

    b.   Cash   2,410,758

            Discount on Bonds Payable   589,242

            Bonds Payable   3,000,000

    c.   Cash   3,000,000

            Premium on Bonds Payable   589,242

            Bonds Payable   2,410,758

    d.   none of the above

8. Several years earlier, the X Corporation issued callable bonds with a face value of $200,000. The bonds could be called at 102. X Corporation has decided to call the bonds at a time when the bonds have a carrying value of $225,000. As a result of the early retirement of the bonds, X Corporation will report _____.

    a. no gain or loss
    b. a loss of $21,000
    c. a gain of $21,000
    d. a loss of $225,000

Use the following information for the next two questions:

On July 1, 1999 Enterprise Company signed a 5-year capital lease on equipment. The terms of the lease require annual payments of $20,000 and the market rate of interest is 10 percent.

9. Which of the following is true?
    a. Enterprise will record a liability of $100,000.
    b. Enterprise will record an asset of $100,000.
    c. Enterprise will record an asset of $75,816.
    d. None of the above is true.

10. What amount will Enterprise report as interest expense on December 31, 1999, the corporate year end?
    a. $3,791
    b. $7,582
    c. $5,000
    d. $10,000

Problem III

Complete the following sentences by filling in the correct response.

1. On an installment note payable, the annual _____ _____ remains the same but _____ _____ becomes smaller each year.

2. When the market rate equals the face rate, the cash proceeds will equal the _____ value of the bond.

3. Premiums are _____ to and discounts are _____ from the face value of a bond in arriving at its carrying value.

4. When the market rate is greater than the face rate, the bond will be issued at a _____.

5. On the cash flow statement, the proceeds of a bond issue will be shown in the _____ section and the payment of interest expense will be shown in the _____ section.

6. When the face rate is _____ than the market rate, the bond will be issued at a premium.

7. A bond that is retired at a price that is greater than its carrying value will result in a _____ being shown on the income statement.

8. A bond may be retired by any one of the following three methods:
   a. _____
   b. _____
   c. _____

9. When bonds are converted to stock, the _____ _____ of the bond is transferred into the _____ _____ account, and no _____ or _____ is recognized.

10. When a company signs a capital lease, it will record an _____ for the leased property and a _____ representing the leasehold obligation.

Problem IV

On May 1, 1996, the Dialex Corporation issued a 3-year $500,000 note payable. The face rate on the note was 8 percent and interest is paid semi-annually. The market rate of interest was 10 percent. The amortization schedule (rounded to the nearest dollar) is as follows:

Date	Cash Payment (.04 x FV)	Interest Expense (.05 x CV)	Discount Amortized	Discount	Note Carrying Value
5/1/96				$25,378	$474,622
11/1/96	$20,000	$23,731	$3,731	$21,647	$478,353
5/1/97	$20,000	$23,918	$3,918	$17,730	$482,270
11/1/97	$20,000	$24,114	$4,114	$13,616	$486,384
5/1/98	$20,000	$24,319	$4,319	$9,297	$490,703
11/1/98	$20,000	$24,535	$4,535	$4,762	$495,238
5/1/99	$20,000	$24,762	$4,762	$0	$500,000

Prepare the following entries in general journal form:
    a. The issuance of the note payable on 5/1/96.
    b. The interest payment on 11/1/97.
    c. The adjusting entry on 12/31/98.

General Journal

Date	Account Title	Debit	Credit

©The McGraw-Hill Companies, Inc., 2000

Problem V

Prepare the following selected journal entries for Kirk Company for 19X2:

1/1 Kirk entered into a 7-year capital lease on $20,000 of equipment. The annual lease payment is $3,841 and the market rate of interest is 8%.

4/1 Kirk made the annual $26,380 payment on a $100,000 installment note payable issued one year earlier. At the time the note was issued, the market rate of interest was 10 percent.

7/1 Kirk issued a $400,000, 8% face rate, 10-year bond payable. The bond pays interest on 7/1 and 12/31 and the market rate of interest is 6%.

12/31 The $16,000 interest payment related to the bond issued on 7/1 was made.

12/31 The lease payment of $3,841 from the 1/1 equipment rental is paid.

General Journal

Date	Account Title	Debit	Credit

Pause and Reflect

A friend with no business experience is excited about the financing she was able to obtain for a new stereo system. Your friend says she signed a $1,500 noninterest-bearing note to be paid at the end of two years. Assuming that the market rate of interest is 12% per annum on similar notes, explain to your friend that the note is not interest free.

Solutions for Chapter 20

Problem I

1. T
2. F
3. T
4. T
5. T
6. T
7. F
8. T
9. F
10. T

Problem II

1. b
2. a
3. c
4. d
5. b
6. a
7. b
8. c
9. c
10. a

Problem III

1. cash payment, interest expense
2. face
3. added, subtracted
4. discount
5. financing, operating
6. greater
7. loss
8. a. Buying the bond in the secondary market.
   b. Using the bond's call feature
   c. Converting the bonds into stock
9. carrying value, common stock, gain, loss
10. asset, liability

Problem IV

	General Journal		
Date	Account Title	Debit	Credit
5/1/96	Cash	474,622	
	Discount on Note Payable	25,378	
	Note Payable		500,000
11/1/97	Interest Expense	24,114	
	Discount on Note Payable		4,114
	Cash		20,000
12/31/98	Interest Expense	8,254	
	Discount on Note Payable		1,587
	Interest Payable		6,667

Adjusting entry on 12/31/98:
  Interest Expense $24,762 X 2/6 = $8,254
  Interest Payable $20,000 X 2/6 = $6,667

Problem V

	General Journal	Debit	Credit
Date	Account Title		
1/1	Equipment	20,000	
	Leasehold Obligation		20,000
4/1	Note Payable	16,380	
	Interest Expense	10,000	
	Cash		26,380
7/1	Cash	459,520	
	Bonds Payable		400,000
	Premium on Bonds Payable		59,520
12/31	Interest Expense	13,786	
	Premium on Bonds Payable	2,214	
	Cash		16,000
12/31	Interest Expense	1,600	
	Leasehold Obligation	2,241	
	Cash		3,841

Cash Proceeds on 6/1 Bond Issue:
  PV(20,3%) X $400,000 =   .5537 X $400,000 = $221,480
  PVa(20,3%) X $16,000 = 14.8775 X $16,000 = $238,040
                                                  $459,520

Interest Expense on 12/31 Bond Payment:
  $459,520 X .06/2 = $13,786

Interest Expense on 12/31 Lease Payment:
  $20,000 X .08 = $1,600

Pause and Reflect

The value of the noninterest-bearing note, and by implication the stereo system, is dependent upon the market rate of interest. The value of the note today is equal to the present value of the note discounted at the market rate of interest. At a 12% market rate of interest, the note has a present value of $1,196. The difference between the present value and the face amount of the note to be repaid in two years is the amount of interest cost incurred. In this case, $304 in interest is being paid for the purchase of the stereo system.

Chapter 21
Recording and Communicating Operational Investment Activities

Chapter Overview

This chapter presents information about plant assets, natural resources, and intangible assets. The chapter explores the process of recording and reporting the acquisition, use and disposal of these assets. Allocating the cost of a plant asset to the periods benefited is called depreciation. For financial reporting purposes depreciation can be calculated using the straight-line method, units-of-production method, or accelerated method. The expense resulting from the cost of natural resources is called depletion. The cost of intangible assets, which have no physical substance, is allocated through a process called amortization.

As you study this chapter, you should first become familiar with which costs should be included in the acquisition cost of operational assets. You also should be able to compute depreciation using the straight-line method, units-of-production method, and accelerated method. When operational assets are disposed of, the cost of the asset and the related accumulated depreciation, depletion, or amortization must be removed from the accounts. You should know how to calculate the gain or loss that will result when the disposal price is different from the carrying value of the asset. Finally, you should be familiar with how operational assets and their related expenses are reported in the financial statements.

Read and Recall Questions

Learning Objective:
L.O.1. Describe the issues involved in determining the cost of plant assets.

What are the three categories of operational assets?

Define plant assets. What are three examples of plant assets?

How does one determine whether to categorize a tangible, long-term asset as a plant asset?

What does it mean to capitalize an expenditure?

Distinguish between a capital expenditure and revenue expenditure.

What items are normally included in the acquisition cost of a building?

What items are normally included in the construction cost of a building?

What items are normally included in the acquisition cost of land?

What items are normally included in the acquisition cost of equipment?

On what grounds may a company choose not to capitalize certain capital expenditures?

Learning Objective:
L.O.2. Explain the nature of depreciation and related issues regarding the use of plant assets.

What is depreciation?

What is accumulated depreciation? What type of account is Accumulated Depreciation?

What is the carrying value or book value of a plant asset?

What factors affect the depreciation calculation?

What causes the useful life of a plant asset to be limited?

What is the salvage or residual value of an asset? What is depreciable cost?

What is straight-line depreciation? How is it calculated?

What is the units-of-production method of depreciation? How is it calculated?

What advantage does units-of-production depreciation have over straight-line depreciation?

What justifies the use of an accelerated depreciation method?

What is declining-balance depreciation? How is double-declining balance depreciation calculated?

Why may companies use a midyear convention for assets purchased or disposed of during the year?

Why may depreciation for tax purposes differ from depreciation for financial reporting purposes?

How do businesses benefit from tax depreciation?

What is the modified accelerated cost recovery system (MACRS)?

How do companies account for the undepreciated cost of an asset when the estimated useful life and/or salvage value have changed?

What are extraordinary repairs and betterments?

Learning Objective:
L.O.3. Determine the financial impact of plant asset disposals.

What three things must the entries associated with the disposal of a plant asset accomplish?

On the exchange of dissimilar assets, how is the gain or loss on the transaction calculated?

Why are gains on the exchange of similar assets not recognized? Why are losses recognized?

What value is assigned to a new asset acquired through the trade-in of a similar asset?

What are the tax effects of an exchange of similar productive assets?

Learning Objective:
L.O.4. Describe the characteristics of natural resources and the process of depletion.

What are natural resources? What items are included in the acquisition cost of natural resources?

What is depletion? How is depletion calculated?

When does depletion cost become an expense?

Learning Objective:
L.O.5. Explain the characteristics of intangible assets and the process of amortization.

What are intangible assets?

What is a patent? What is a patent's legal life? What is included in the cost of a patent?

What is a copyright? What is included in the cost of a copyright? What is the legal life of a copyright?

What is a franchise?

What is a leasehold? A leasehold improvement?

What is goodwill? When can goodwill be recognized? How is it calculated?

What is amortization? How is amortization calculated?

> **Learning Objective:**
> L.O.6. Illustrate how to communicate events involving operational investments to external and internal users.

Why do companies maintain subsidiary records of operational assets?

Why should external users be interested in the depreciation method used for financial reporting purposes?

What information about operational assets will be included in the notes to the financial statements?

What information about operational assets will appear on the income statement?

What information about operational assets will appear on the cash flows statement?

Why may a company have the motivation to improperly capitalize expenditures?

Outline of Key Concepts

I. The acquisition of operational investments involves a capital expenditure.
   A. Plant assets are tangible assets held primarily for use in a business for more than one accounting period.
      1. Includes land, buildings, and equipment.
      2. Also called property, plant, and equipment.
   B. Accounting for capital expenditures and revenue expenditures differs.
      1. Capital expenditures.
         a. Create the expectation of future benefits that apply beyond the current accounting period.
         b. Are capitalized--add the cost of the plant asset to the asset account rather than expense it immediately.
      2. Revenue expenditures.
         a. Provide benefits exclusively during the current accounting period.
         b. Are generally expensed when incurred.
   C. The cost of any purchased plant asset includes all normal, reasonable, and necessary expenditures to acquire the asset and prepare it for its intended use.
      1. When land and depreciable assets are acquired with one purchase price, the buyer must allocate the total purchase price between them.
         a. Allocations are frequently based on appraisal values.
      2. Cost of equipment normally includes the purchase price, freight charges, sales taxes paid, and installation costs.
   D. Materiality relates to whether an item's dollar amount or its inherent nature is significant enough to influence a financial statement user's decisions.

1. If an amount of a capital expenditure is not significant, the expenditure is often expensed.

II. Accounting for the use of plant assets.
   A. Depreciation is the allocation of the acquisition cost of the plant asset over the useful life of the asset.
      1. Asset cost less accumulated depreciation equals the carrying value or book value of the asset.
      2. Carrying value does not measure a decreasing value; it represents the remaining undepreciated cost of the asset.
   B. Four factors affect depreciation calculations.
      1. Cost of the asset.
      2. Useful life--period of time over which a business expects to obtain economic benefits from the use of the plant asset or any other operational investment.
         a. Limited by physical wear and tear or time and obsolescence.
      3. Salvage value--expected fair market value of a plant asset at the end of its useful life.
         a. Cost - Salvage value = Depreciable cost
      4. Method of depreciation.
   C. Three common methods of depreciation are utilized by companies.
      1. Straight-line method--allocates the depreciable cost of the asset to depreciation expense equally over its useful life.
         a. (Cost-Salvage)/Estimated years in useful life = Annual depreciation expense.
         b. Based on the assumption that benefits derived from an asset are constant during each year of its life.
      2. Units-of-production method--depreciation expense is based on actual usage rather than the passage of time.
         a. Useful life is expressed in terms of expected units of output.
         b. Involves a two-step calculation.
            i. (Cost - Salvage value)/Estimated total output = Depreciation per unit of output.
            ii. Depreciation per unit of output x Actual output for current period = Depreciation expense for the current period.
      3. Accelerated depreciation methods recognize relatively greater expense in the early years of the asset's use and progressively less expense as time passes.
         a. Declining-balance depreciation--reflects depreciation expense for each year based on a constant percentage of a declining balance equal to the remaining undepreciated cost of the asset at the start of each year.
   D. Businesses benefit from tax depreciation.
      1. Depreciation expense requires no cash payment; however, the expense reduces taxable income which reduces income taxes paid by the business.
      2. Modified accelerated cost recovery system (MACRS) is the current tax depreciation system.

        a. It specifies the useful lives of and depreciation rates for depreciable assets.
    E. There are numerous issues related to the use of plant assets.
       1. Revisions to the original useful life and salvage value assigned to plant assets require the recalculation of depreciation expense for the current and remaining future periods.
       2. Assets may continue to be used after they are fully depreciated.
           a. The company must stop recording annual depreciation expense.
       3. Extraordinary repairs are capital expenditures that extend the remaining useful life of an operational asset.
       4. Betterments represent capital expenditures to improve the asset's performance capabilities.

III. Plant assets may be discarded, sold, or exchanged for another asset.
    A. Disposals of plant assets generally require entries to accomplish three things.
       1. Record partial-year depreciation expense up to the date of disposal.
       2. Remove the cost of the asset and its related accumulated depreciation from the accounting records.
       3. Record any gain or loss on the disposal of the asset.
    B. Companies may exchange plant assets for other noncash assets.
       1. Gain or loss on the exchange of dissimilar assets is calculated as the difference between the carrying value of the asset given up and whichever of the following two values can be determined more objectively.
           a. Fair market value of the asset received in the exchange.
           b. Fair market value of the asset given up in the exchange.
       2. The exchange of similar assets is not viewed as the culmination of the earnings process.
           a. As a result, accountants do not record any gains determined by a comparison of the fair market value and carrying value of the assets given up.
           b. Losses are recognized and recorded.
           c. On trade-ins, the gain or loss on disposal of the old asset is measured as the difference between the carrying value of the old asset and the trade-in allowance assigned to it in the exchange transaction.
              i. Losses are recognized, gains are not.
              ii. The new asset's carrying value is increased by the amount of any cash given in the exchange.
           d. Gains or loses on the exchange of similar assets are not reported on a company's tax returns.

IV. Natural resources are nonrenewable assets such as coal mines and oil rights.
    A. Cost of the initial investment follows the same general guidelines used for assigning costs to plant assets.
    B. Depletion--allocation of the cost of natural resources as expense over the periods they benefit.
       1. Generally calculated using the units-of-production method.

2. Recorded depletion is not immediately expensed.
3. Depletion is added to the cost of the company's inventory of natural resource.
   i. When the natural resource is sold, depletion is included as a component of cost of goods sold.

V. Intangible assets convey legal rights or benefits to their owner.
   A. Patent--legal right to the commercial benefits of a specified product or process.
      1. Legal life of 17 years; useful economic life may be much shorter.
      2. Cost includes purchase price and legal fees.
         a. Research and development costs cannot be included in the cost of internally created patents.
   B. Copyright--exclusive right for the reproduction and sale of a literary or artistic work.
      1. Legal life is life of the creator plus 50 years; economic useful life is often much shorter.
      2. In many cases, only purchased copyrights are capitalized as assets.
   C. Franchise--exclusive right to operate or sell a brand name product or service in a specified territory.
   D. Leasehold--conveyed by a lease to use equipment, land, and/or buildings for a specified period of time.
   E. Goodwill--represents the value assigned to a purchased company's ability to generate an above average return on invested capital.
      1. Companies record goodwill only when they pay for it as part of the purchase price to acquire another company.
      2. The amount of goodwill purchased is equal to the difference between the total price paid to purchase the company and the value of the purchased company's underlying net assets (all identifiable assets minus liabilities).
      3. Internally generated goodwill is not recorded.
   F. Amortization is the process of allocating the cost of intangible assets to expense over the periods they benefit.
      1. Use the straight-line method.
      2. Amortize the full cost of the asset; no salvage value is used.
      3. Maximum useful life must not exceed 40 years.

VI. Issues related to the reporting of operational investments.
    A. Internally, companies must maintain a separate record for each individual asset.
    B. Financial statements disclose information to external users.
       1. Balance sheet reports all operational assets and discloses the methods of depreciation.
       2. Income statement reports depreciation expense and the gains and losses from disposal of operational investments.
       3. The statement of cash flows reports the amount of cash used and provided by the acquisition and disposal of operational investments.

Problem I

Indicate whether the following statements are either true (T) or false (F).

_____ 1. Annual repairs will be considered capital expenditures.
_____ 2. Installation costs of equipment will be capitalized.
_____ 3. Research and development costs are capitalized and included as assets on the balance sheet.
_____ 4. Depreciation represents the decline in value of the asset during the year.
_____ 5. A company must use the same method of depreciation for both book and tax purposes.
_____ 6. An extraordinary repair may be expensed in the year paid.
_____ 7. A sale of a plant asset at an amount that is greater than its book value, will result in the recognition of a gain.
_____ 8. Both gains and losses are recognized on the exchange of dissimilar assets.
_____ 9. The economic life of a patent may be less than 17 years.
_____ 10. A franchise is considered an intangible asset.

Problem II

Indicate the correct answer by circling the appropriate letter.

1. Maxex Corporation purchased a building and land for $180,000. The land had been appraised for $40,000 and the building for $160,000. What amount will Maxex use in calculating its annual depreciation on the building?
   a. $160,000
   b. $180,000
   c. $144,000
   d. $120,000

Use the following information for the next two questions:
X Corporation purchased a machine for $55,000. The machine has a useful life of 5 years and an expected salvage value of $5,000.

2. What will depreciation expense be for year three under the straight-line method?
   a. $8,000
   b. $10,000
   c. $11,000
   d. $15,000

3. What will depreciation expense be for year one under the double-declining balance method?
   a. $10,000
   b. $12,000
   c. $20,000
   d. $22,000

4. Company Y purchased equipment for $21,000. The equipment was expected to produce 4,000 units over its life and have a salvage value of $1,000. Two hundred units were produced in year one. What amount of depreciation expense will be reported if the units-of-production method is used?
   a. $200
   b. $1,000
   c. $3,000
   d. $4,000

5. Z Corporation sold equipment for $26,000. The equipment originally cost $40,000 and $15,000 of depreciation had been recorded up to the date of the sale. Which of the following is true?
   a. The equipment account will be reduced by $40,000.
   b. Z Corporation will report a $1,000 gain on the sale.
   c. Accumulated depreciation will be reduced by $15,000.
   d. All of the above are true.

6. Sunshine Bullion purchased a gold mine for $3,000,000. The mine is estimated to contain 15,000 ounces of gold. The residual value after extraction of the ore is expected to be $300,000. During the first year of operations, 3,000 ounces of gold were extracted from the mine and sold. Cost of goods sold will be _____.
   a. $265,000
   b. $540,000
   c. $300,000
   d. $600,000

7. On January 1, 19X1, Acquisition Inc. purchased a company in a transaction that resulted in the recording of $2,000,000 of goodwill. What amount of amortization expense will be recorded each year by the company if amortized over the maximum time permitted by GAAP?
   a. $200,000
   b. $100,000
   c. $50,000
   d. $25,000

8. Z Corporation purchased a machine for $100,000. The machine has a useful life of 10 years and an expected salvage value of $15,000. What will depreciation expense be for year two under the double declining balance method?
   a. $20,000
   b. $16,000
   c. $14,000
   d. $17,000

9. Ktar Corporation purchased a patent for $320,000 on July 1, 1999. The patent has a remaining legal life of 12 years but management expects its useful life to only be 8 years. What amount will Ktar report as amortization expense for 1999?
   a. $40,000
   b. $26,667
   c. $20,000
   d. $13,333

10. LL Corporation purchased equipment for $40,000 on April 1, 1999. The equipment has a useful life of 4 years and an expected salvage value of $4,000. Assuming that LL Corporation uses the mid-year convention, what will depreciation expense be for 1999 under the straight-line method?
   a. $9,000
   b. $6,750
   c. $5,000
   d. $4,500

11. Which of the following would not be considered an intangible asset?
   a. goodwill
   b. franchises
   c. leasehold improvements
   d. all of the above are intangible assets

12. The purchase of equipment will be shown in the _____ section of the cash flow statement.
   a. operating
   b. investing
   c. financing
   d. non-cash activities

Problem III

Following is a list of important ideas and key concepts from the chapter. To test your knowledge of these terms, match the term with the definition by placing the number in the space provided.

_____ accelerated depreciation
_____ amortization
_____ betterments
_____ capital expenditure
_____ capitalize
_____ copyright
_____ depreciable cost
_____ depletion
_____ extraordinary repairs
_____ franchise
_____ goodwill

_____ leasehold
_____ leasehold improvement
_____ materiality
_____ midyear convention
_____ natural resources
_____ operational investments
_____ patent
_____ plant assets
_____ revenue expenditure
_____ salvage value
_____ useful life

1. An intangible asset giving its owner the exclusive legal right to the commercial benefits of a specified product or process.

2. The period of time over which a business expects to obtain economic benefits from the use of an operational investment.

3. An intangible asset representing the value assigned to a purchased company's ability to generate an above average return on invested capital.

4. An accounting concept that relates to whether an item's dollar amount or its inherent nature is significant enough to influence a financial statement user.

5. Capital expenditures that improve an asset's performance capabilities.

6. An intangible asset that gives its owner the exclusive legal right for the reproduction and sale of a literary or artistic work.

7. Tangible assets acquired primarily for use in a business over a time span covering more than one accounting period.

8. The convention that reflects depreciation expense for each asset as if it were purchased or disposed of exactly halfway through the company's fiscal year.

9. A method of depreciation that recognizes relatively greater expense in early years of asset use and progressively less expense as time passes.

10. An intangible asset representing the amounts paid by a lessee to make physical improvements that are an integral part of leased property.

11. The process of allocating the cost of natural resources to an expense over the periods they benefit.

12. To add an expenditure to the cost of an asset, rather than expensing it immediately.

13. Nonrenewable assets such as coal mines or oil rights.

14. The expected fair market value of a plant asset at the end of its useful life. Also referred to as residual value.

15. An intangible asset representing the exclusive right to operate or sell a brand name product in a specified territory.

16. The process of allocating the cost of intangible assets to an expense over the periods they benefit.

17. An intangible asset conveyed by a lease to use equipment, land, and/or buildings for a specified period of time.

18. An expenditure that creates the expectation of future benefits that apply beyond the current accounting period.

19. Long-term investments made to acquire the facilities necessary for the conduct of basic business activities.

20. An expenditure that provides benefits exclusively during the current accounting period.

21. Expenditures that extend the remaining useful life of an operational investment.

22. The portion of a plant asset's total cost that will be depreciated over its useful life.

©The McGraw-Hill Companies, Inc., 2000

Problem IV

Complete the following sentences by filling in the correct response.

1. A capital expenditure creates the expectation of a _____ benefit.

2. The expected value of a plant asset at the end of its useful life is referred to as the _____ value.

3. A plant asset's _____ less its _____ _____ equals the depreciable cost.

4. _____ repairs extend the useful life of an asset and _____ represent capital expenditures that improve the asset's performance capabilities.

5. The accounting concept of _____ causes _____ but not _____ to be recognized on the exchange of similar assets.

6. Intangibles are amortized using the _____ method over their _____ _____ but not to exceed _____ years.

Problem V

Prepare the necessary journal entries for the following selected property transactions:

a) A patent with an estimated useful life of 10 years is purchased for $160,000.

b) Equipment originally costing $45,000 with $38,000 of accumulated depreciation is discarded as worthless.

c) Machinery originally costing $100,000 with $65,000 of accumulated depreciation is sold for $41,000.

d) The company traded a delivery truck that originally cost $22,000 (accumulated depreciation of $16,000) for a new delivery truck. The new truck cost $26,000. The company was given a trade-in allowance on the old truck of $9,000 and paid $17,000 in cash.

e) The patent acquired in (a) above was used for 3 months during the year.

Problem V (continued)

General Journal

Date	Account Title	Debit	Credit

Pause and Reflect

Assume that two companies, Alpha and Omega, each purchased a new high-speed color copier for $25,000. Both companies estimate that the useful life of the copier will be four years, and it will have a salvage value of $4,000. Alpha Company has decided to use the straight-line method while Omega Company has elected to use the double-declining balance method. Depreciation expense for both companies is reported below. Accountants for both companies have indicated that the method selected is acceptable for reporting depreciation expense on the copier. How can each company's accountants be correct?

	Alpha Company Straight-Line Method	Omega Company Double-Declining Balance
Year 1	$5,250	$12,500
Year 2	$5,250	$ 6,250
Year 3	$5,250	$ 2,250
Year 4	$5,250	$ - 0 -

Solutions for Chapter 21

Problem I

1. F
2. T
3. F
4. F
5. F
6. F
7. T
8. T
9. T
10. T

Problem II

1. c
2. b
3. d
4. b
5. d
6. b
7. c
8. b
9. c
10. d
11. d
12. b

Problem III

9	accelerated depreciation	17	leasehold
16	amortization	10	leasehold improvement
5	betterments	4	materiality
18	capital expenditure	8	midyear convention
12	capitalize	13	natural resources
6	copyright	19	operational investments
22	depreciable cost	1	patent
11	depletion	7	plant assets
21	extraordinary repairs	20	revenue expenditure
15	franchise	14	salvage value
3	goodwill	2	useful life

Problem IV

1. future
2. salvage or residual
3. cost, salvage value
4. Extraordinary, betterments
5. conservatism, losses, gains
6. straight-line, useful lives, 40

Problem V

Date	General Journal Account Title	Debit	Credit
a)	Patent	160,000	
	Cash		160,000
b)	Loss on disposal	7,000	
	Accumulated depreciation	38,000	
	Equipment		45,000
c)	Cash	41,000	
	Accumulated depreciation	65,000	
	Machinery		100,000
	Gain on sale		6,000
d)	Truck (new)	23,000	
	Accumulated depreciation	16,000	
	Truck (old)		22,000
	Cash		17,000
e)	Amortization expense - Patent	4,000	
	Patent		4,000
	($160,000/10 = 16,000 per year) X 3/12		

Pause and Reflect

The accountants for both companies are indeed correct in their assertions. Either depreciation method, straight-line or double-declining balance, is acceptable for financial statement reporting purposes. Each company has selected the depreciation method that, in its view, most closely matches benefits received with expenses recognized in all periods. Alpha Company has assumed that each year will benefit uniformly from the services of the copier. On the other hand, Omega Company could be expecting greater benefits early in the life of the copier and may also expect maintenance costs of operating the copier to increase as the copier ages. By using an accelerated depreciation method, Omega may be attempting to maintain total copier operating expenses at a relatively level amount each period.

©The McGraw-Hill Companies, Inc., 2000

Chapter 22
Recording and Communicating Nonoperational Investment Activities

Chapter Overview

Chapter 22 presents the process for recording and communicating nonoperational investment activities. Companies make investments in equity and debt securities to enhance their overall net income through dividend and interest income. The type of securities purchased and the existence of influence or control over the investee's operations determine how a company reports these investments. The chapter discusses the characteristics and accounting for trading securities, available-for-sale securities, and held-to-maturity securities. Chapter 22 also presents the equity method of accounting for equity securities which is used when an investor owns from 20 to 50 percent of the investee's voting stock. Consolidated financial statements are also illustrated in the chapter.

As you study this chapter, you will note that the investor's intent and level of influence over the investee's operations play a significant role in how investments in equity and debt securities are recorded and reported. When studying trading securities and available-for-sale securities, pay close attention to the reporting of the unrealized holdings gains and losses; the manner of reporting differs between these two classifications of investments. Seek to understand the rationale for the equity method of accounting for investments in equity securities. The recording and reporting of equity method securities will be easier to remember if you can think through the conceptual basis of the method.

Read and Recall Questions

Learning Objective:
L.O.1. Describe how to account for investments that give a corporation significant influence or control over another corporation.

Why do corporations invest in the equity and debt securities of other corporations?

What are the three categories of ownership used to determine the appropriate accounting for investments in the equity securities of another corporation?

What are consolidated financial statements? When must consolidated financial statements be prepared?

Distinguish between the parent company and subsidiary company.

Why should transactions between the parent company and subsidiary company be eliminated in the consolidation process?

When is the equity method of accounting for investments used? Describe the equity method.

When the equity method is used, what effect does the investee's net income have on the investor's investment account? What effect do dividends have on the investor's investment account?

When the equity method is used, what does the investor's investment account equal? Explain.

What is mark-to-market accounting? Why does mark-to-market accounting for equity and some debt securities help financial statement users?

Learning Objective:
L.O.2. Explain why investments are classified as trading securities and how to account for and communicate transactions involving these investments.

What are trading securities? Why would a company invest in trading securities?

How would dividends received from investments in trading securities be accounted for?

How are realized gains and losses from the sale of trading securities calculated and reported?

Is the mark-to-market method of investment valuation applied to individual equity securities or to the portfolio of investments? Explain.

What is a market adjustment account? When is it used?

When would the market adjustment account have a credit balance? A debit balance?

How do purchases and sales of individual debt and equity securities affect the market adjustment account?

On which financial statement are the unrealized gains and losses on trading securities reported?

Learning Objective:
L.O.3. Describe why investments are classified as available-for-sale securities and how to record and communicate transactions involving these investments.

What are available-for-sale securities?

How are the gains and losses that result from adjusting available-for-sale securities to market value reported?

For available-for-sale securities, what does the Net Unrealized Gain or Loss account represent?

What is the rationale for dividing investments into trading securities and available-for-sale securities?

If a corporation has an investment in the preferred stock of another company, how will the investor company account for the investment?

Learning Objective:
L.O.4. Explain the importance of investments in debt securities and how to account for and communicate transactions involving these investments.

What are the differences between investments in debt and equity securities?

What are held-to-maturity securities?

What factors determine the cash paid for debt instruments?

Is accrued interest included in the cost of debt securities? Explain.

Does the purchaser of a noninterest-bearing note use a discount account to show the difference between the face value and purchase price of the note? Why?

If an investor sells a noninterest-bearing note before its maturity date, how is the difference between the cash proceeds and the face value of the note accounted for?

If an investor holds interest-bearing notes as trading securities, will any discount or premium be amortized when cash interest is received? Why?

When an investor purchases bonds as available-for-sale securities, how is the price paid for the bonds determined?

If an investor holds bonds as available-for-sale securities, will any discount or premium be amortized when cash interest is received? Why?

If an investor purchases bonds between interest payment dates, how is the accrued interest recorded?

If an investor holds bonds as held-to-maturity securities, how is any discount or premium accounted for?

How does the reporting of bonds classified as held-to-maturity securities differ from bonds held as available-for-sale securities?

Learning Objective:
L.O.5. Illustrate how companies report their investment activities to interested users.

Why are external users interested in a company's investment in debt and equity securities?

What are internal users interested in a company's investment in debt and equity securities?

How are trading securities reported on the balance sheet? How are available-for-sale securities reported on the balance sheet? How are held-to-maturity securities reported on the balance sheet? How are investments in equity securities with significant influence reported?

In what three ways may a company's investments affect its income statement?

How do a company's investments in debt and equity securities affect the cash flows statement?

Outline of Key Concepts

I. Investments in equity securities may be acquired to obtain a significant influence in or control of another corporation.
   A. Effective control is achieved when the investment of one company exceeds 50 percent of the voting stock of another company.
      1. Parent company--the controlling company.
         a. The investment account will be maintained using the equity method.
      2. Subsidiary company--the investee firm.
      3. Legal distinctions between the parent and subsidiary are usually ignored for reporting purposes.
      4. Consolidated financial statements are prepared as if the two companies were one economic unit.
         a. Economic transactions between the parent and subsidiary should be eliminated.
   B. Significant influence is assumed with ownership of between 20 and 50 percent of a company's voting stock, unless there is evidence to the contrary.
      1. Investor company must use the equity method to account for these investments.
         a. Investor records its proportionate share of the investee's net income as an increase in the value of the investment account.
         b. Investor records the dividends it receives as a decrease in the investment account.
         c. The equity method violates historical cost principle, but it better reflects the investor's changing financial interest in the investee corporation's net assets.
         d. The investor's investment account equals the investor's share of the investee's stockholders' equity.

II. Trading securities are debt and equity securities that companies purchase with the intent of selling them after holding them for a short period of time.
   A. Equity securities--the cost of the securities includes the brokerage fees paid to acquire the stock.
      1. Cash dividends are recorded as revenue when they are received.
      2. Gains or losses realized through the sale of equity investments are computed on the basis of the carrying cost of the securities held compared to the net proceeds from the sale.
   B. Mark-to-market accounting is used to report trading securities.
      1. The investment portfolio is reported at the equivalent market value at the time financial statements are issued.
      2. Market adjustment account--reflects the adjustments made to the total cost of the trading securities to show the total fair value of the securities.
         a. Therefore, trading securities are reported in the current assets section of the balance sheet at their fair value.

      Trading securities at purchase price
     - <u>Market Adjustment</u>
      Trading securities at fair value
   b. Unrealized losses represent a decrease in the fair value of the portfolio of trading securities while unrealized gains reflect the increase in the fair value of the portfolio of trading securities.
     i. Unrealized gains or losses are reported on the income statement.

III. Available-for-sale (AFS) securities are debt and equity securities which companies purchase in order to maintain a portfolio of securities that management can sell, as needed, to raise cash for particular projects.
 A. They are typically reported as long-term investments.
 B. Available-for-sale equity securities are reported on a fair value basis.
  1. Similar to trading securities, a market adjustment is used to report the fair value of the portfolio of securities.
  2. Unrealized gains or losses are recorded in the Net Unrealized Gain or Loss account.
   a. This account reflects the adjustments made to total stockholders' equity.
   b. This account will not be reported on the income statement.
   c. The unrealized gains or losses are not reported in net income because the investment is not held for generating returns but to build or support relationships.

IV. Debt securities can be classified as trading securities, available-for-sale securities, or held-to-maturity securities.
 A. Debt securities classified as trading securities usually consist of noninterest-bearing and interest-bearing notes.
  1. Noninterest-bearing notes--purchase price is the present value of the promised future cash flows at the market rate of interest.
   a. No discount account is used.
   b. Interest earned is equal to the difference between the note's purchase price and its face amount upon maturity.
   c. If the note is sold before maturity, the difference between the proceeds of the sale and the purchase price is either a gain or a loss.
  2. Interest-bearing notes--purchase price depends upon whether the market interest rate at the time of the investment is greater or less than the face interest rate.
   a. The premium or discount is not recorded separately, and it is not amortized because the company does not intend to hold the note to maturity.
   b. If the debt security is acquired between interest dates, the purchasing company excludes the accrued interest from the cost of the investment because it will received the accrued interest as part of the cash interest at the next interest payment date.

©The McGraw-Hill Companies, Inc., 2000

        c. When an interest-bearing note is sold between its interest dates, the gain or loss on the sale of an interest-bearing note is the difference between the cost of the debt security and the net sales price of the debt instrument.
            i. Net sales price is the quoted sale price of the security less the brokerage fee.
     3. Mark-to-market accounting is used to report debt securities classified as trading securities.
        a. See the discussion under equity securities classified as trading securities.
  B. Debt securities classified as available-for-sale securities usually consist of bonds.
     1. Purchase price is the present value of the promised future cash flows at the market interest rate.
     2. Because these bonds will not be sold in the near future, firms are interested in the effective interest rate on these bonds.
        a. Therefore, firms amortize the premiums and discounts on these bonds and maintain each debt security on an amortized cost basis.
        b. A separate discount or premium account is not usually used.
     3. Gains or losses on the sale of the securities are determined by comparing the amortized cost on the date of the sale with the cash proceeds of the sale.
     4. Available-for-sale debt securities are reported on a fair value basis.
        a. See the discussion under equity securities classified as available-for-sale securities.
  C. Held-to-maturity securities consist only of debt securities that a firm buys with the intent to hold until they mature.
     1. The purchaser amortizes any premium or discount on individual debt instruments to generate the effective interest earned during the accounting period.
        a. Entries are the same as available-for-sale securities.
     2. These securities are reported as long-term assets in the investments section of the balance sheet.
        a. They are reported at their amortized cost because they will not be sold before their maturity date.

V. Reporting investments.
  A. Investments are reported externally through the financial statements.
     1. Balance sheet--investments in debt and equity securities are reported as current or long-term investments.
        a. Trading securities--reported at their fair value as current assets.
        b. Available-for-sale and held-to-maturity securities that mature in the coming year are also classified as current assets.
        c. Investments section reports the fair value of available-for-sale securities, the amortized cost of held-to-maturity securities, and the carrying value of the investments that have a significant influence in another company.
     2. Income statement--there are four ways investments may affect the income statement.

    a. Realized gains and losses from the sale of securities held as investments.
    b. Unrealized holding gains or losses on trading securities.
    c. Permanent declines in the fair value of available-for-sale securities.
    d. Investment revenue (dividends or interest).
  3. Cash flows statement--the investing section reflects the amount of cash paid and received as a result of the company's investing activities.
B. Internal reports must help financial mangers make decisions about specific securities as well as portfolios of securities.
  1. Accounting system must reflect information about the cost of each security purchased and its performance.
  2. Financial managers use the information to assess whether the risk assumed is justified by the returns being generated by the investment.

Problem I

Indicate whether the following statements are either true (T) or false (F).

_____1. If significant influence (but not control) is exerted over another corporation, the equity method will be used to account for the investment.
_____2. An unrealized loss on the decline in fair market value of available-for-sale securities will be shown on the income statement.
_____3. An investment classified as a trading security will be shown as a current asset on the balance sheet.
_____4. Held-to-maturity securities will generally be classified as long-term investments and will be reported at their amortized cost.
_____5. An investment classified as a trading security will be shown at its historical cost.
_____6. An unrealized gain on an increase in the market value of a trading security will be shown on the income statement.
_____7. Held-to-maturity securities may contain investments in both stocks and bonds.
_____8. If a company exerts significant influence over another corporation, the investment will be carried at fair market value.
_____9. The Market Adjustment account may have either a debit or credit balance.
_____10. Consolidated financial statements are the combined financial statements of a parent and a subsidiary.

Problem II

Indicate the correct answer by circling the appropriate letter.

1. On December 31, prior to any adjusting entry, Y Corporation showed a $1,167,000 balance in its Trading Securities account and a debit balance of $123,000 in its Market Adjustment - TS account. Which of the following is true if the trading securities have a fair market value of $1,100,000 as of December 31?
   a. Y Corporation will report an unrealized loss of $67,000.
   b. Y Corporation will report an unrealized loss of $190,000.
   c. Y Corporation will report a net current asset of $1,167,000 on the balance sheet.
   d. Both b and c are correct.

Use the following information for the next two questions:
On January 1, 19X1, X Corporation purchased 20 percent of the outstanding stock of Target Corporation for $560,000. During 19X1, Target reported net income of $120,000 and paid a total cash dividend to all stockholders of $20,000.

2. Assume that X Corporation does not exert significant influence over Target Corporation. What effect will the above events have on X Corporation's net income before taxes for 19X1?
   a. Increase by $4,000
   b. Increase by $20,000
   c. Increase by $28,000
   d. Increase by $140,000

3. Assume that X Corporation exerts significant influence over Target Corporation. What effect will the above events have on X Corporation's net income before taxes for 19X1?
   a. Increase by $4,000
   b. Increase by $20,000
   c. Increase by $24,000
   d. Increase by $140,000

4. On July 1, X Corporation purchased bonds with a face value of $100,000 and carrying a face rate of 8 percent. The bonds mature in 10 years and interest is paid each July 1 and December 31. On the date of the purchase, the market rate of interest was 10 percent. If the bonds are classified as available-for-sale securities, what amount will X Corporation report as an asset on the date of the purchase?
   a. $83,579
   b. $87,538
   c. $92,781
   d. $100,000

5. Assume the same fact as the previous question except that the bonds are purchased on August 1 at 88. What will be the total cash payment for the purchase of the bonds?
   a. $88,667
   b. $89,137
   c. $100,000
   d. $100,667

6. On June 1, ACQ Corporation purchased 65 percent of the outstanding stock of Target Corporation for $3,000,000. Which of the following statements is true regarding the acquisition of Target Corporation?
   a. The two companies will prepare consolidated financial statements.
   b. The purchase will be classified as a trading security on the balance sheet.
   c. The purchase will be classified as an available-for-sale security on the balance sheet.
   d. ACQ will use the equity method to account for the purchase of stock.

7. On January 1, 19X5, Cortex Corporation purchased 40 percent of the outstanding stock of Target Corporation for $800,000. During 19X5, Target reported net income of $100,000 and paid a total cash dividend to all stockholders of $30,000. Under the equity method of accounting, the Investment in Target Corporation Stock account balance at the end of the year will be _____.
   a. $800,000
   b. $930,000
   c. $852,000
   d. $828,000

8. On March 31, Z Corporation purchased a non-interest bearing U.S. Treasury bill with a face value of $20,000 for $18,900. The investment was classified as a trading security and was sold later in the year for $19,200. On the date of the sale Z Corporation will recognize a/an _____.
   a. unrealized gain of $300
   b. gain on sale of $300
   c. interest income of $300
   d. none of the above

9. XYZ Corporation purchased stock in ABC Corporation which is classified as an available-for-sale security. During the year, ABC paid a $12,000 dividend to XYZ. The journal entry to record the dividend will be _____.
    a.   Cash $12,000
           AFS-ABC Corporation $12,000
    b.   AFS-ABC Corporation $12,000
           Dividend income $12,000
    c.   Cash $12,000
           Dividend income $12,000
    d.   Cash $12,000
           Investment in Stock $12,000

10. Which of the following investments are not adjusted to fair market value at the time the financial statements are prepared?
    a. investments in debt securities classified as trading securities
    b. investments in equity securities classified as available-for-sale securities
    c. investments in equity securities where the equity method is used to account for the investment
    d. investments in debt securities classified as available-for-sale securities

11. Investments in equity securities will be shown in the _____ section of the cash flow statement.
    a. operating
    b. investing
    c. financing
    d. non-cash activities

12. The receipt of a dividend from an equity investment classified as an available-for-sale security will be shown in the _____ section of the cash flow statement.
    a. operating
    b. investing
    c. financing
    d. non-cash activities

Problem III

Following is a list of important ideas and key concepts from the chapter. To test your knowledge of these terms, match the term with the definition by placing the number in the space provided.

_____ available-for-sale securities _____ market adjustment account
_____ equity method _____ parent company
_____ held-to-maturity securities _____ subsidiary company
_____ mark to market _____ trading securities

1. An investor company that owns more than 50 percent of another corporation's voting stock

2. Debt and equity securities bought with the intent of maintaining a portfolio of securities that management can sell, as needed, to raise cash for particular projects

3. The accounting method used by an investor company that exercises a significant influence over an investee company's operations and which reflects increases and decreases in the investment account of the investor company in proportion to the investee's stockholders equity

4. Debt securities the firm buys with the intent of holding until they mature

5. An investee company that has more than 50 percent of its voting stock owned by another company

6. A balance sheet account that reflects adjustments made to the total cost of trading securities and available-for-sale securities to show the fair value of the securities' portfolio

7. Debt and equity securities bought with the intent of selling the securities after holding them for a short period of time

8. A method of showing the fair value of the entire portfolio of trading securities and available-for-sale securities on the balance sheet without altering the cost of the individual securities

Problem IV

1. Prepare the necessary journal entries for the securities transactions in the general journal provided on the following page:

   a) Acme sold a non-interest bearing U.S. Treasury Bill for $11,000. The security is classified as a trading security and originally cost $9,700.

   b) A cash dividend of $300 was received on a common stock investment that is classified as a trading security.

   c) Acme purchased $300,000 of the stock of Elway Corporation. The stock is classified as an available-for-sale security.

   d) Acme received a $10,000 cash dividend from Target Company. Acme had acquired a 40 percent interest (significant influence) in Target two years earlier.

   e) Target Company reported a net loss of $100,000 for the year.

   f) The portfolio of trading securities has a cost of $456,000 and a fair value of $412,000 at the end of the year. At the end of the preceding year, Market Adjustment - TS had a $11,000 credit balance.

   g) The fair value of the Elway Corporation stock at the end of the year is $315,000.

2. Acme's net income will increase/<decrease> by _____ as a result of the preceding securities transactions.

Problem IV (continued)

Date	Account Title	Debit	Credit

Problem V

During the year, FX Company had the following transactions (only investments held):

January 1	Purchased 23 percent of the outstanding stock of X Company for $2,100,000.
March 12	X Company paid a $43,000 dividend to FX Company
December 31	X Company reported net income of $200,000
December 31	The market value of FX's investment in X Company stock is $2,440,000.

Required: Prepare the necessary journal entries under the following assumptions:

    a. FX does not exert significant influence over the operations of X Company.
    b. FX exerts significant influence over the operations of X Company.

General Journal

Date	Account Title	Debit	Credit

Pause and Reflect

Supertech Company just released its most recent financial statements. The investments sections of its balance sheet reported long-term investments at an amount of $2,734,000. Supertech's long-term investments include available-for-sale investments, held-to-maturity investments, and a subsidiary over which it has significant influence. What is the reporting basis for the aggregate investment of $2,734,000?

Solutions for Chapter 22

Problem I

1. T
2. F
3. T
4. T
5. F
6. T
7. F
8. F
9. T
10. T

Problem II

1. b
2. a
3. c
4. b
5. a
6. a
7. d
8. b
9. c
10. c
11. b
12. a

Problem III

2	available-for-sale securities	6	market adjustment account
3	equity method	1	parent company
4	held-to-maturity securities	5	subsidiary company
8	mark to market	7	trading securities

Problem IV

1.

General Journal

Date	Account Title	Debit	Credit
a)	Cash	11,000	
	Trading Securities - U.S. Treasury Bills		9,700
	Gain on Sale of U.S. Treasury Bills		1,300
b)	Cash	300	
	Dividend Revenue		300
c)	Available-for-sale-Securities Elway	300,000	
	Cash		300,000
d)	Cash	10,000	
	Investment in Target Company Stock		10,000
e)	Investment Loss	40,000	
	Investment in Target Company Stock		40,000
f)	Unrealized Loss	33,000	
	Market Adjustment - TS		33,000
g)	Market Adjustment - Available-for-sale	15,000	
	Unrealized gain or loss		15,000

2. The company's net income will go down by $71,400 calculated as follows:

    a) $ 1,300
    b)   300
    e)   < 40,000>
    f)   < 33,000>
           <$71,400>

Problem V

General Journal

Date	Account Title	Debit	Credit
Part a.			
1/1	Availabe-for-Sale-X Company	2,100,000	
	Cash		2,100,000
3/12	Cash	43,000	
	Dividend income		43,000
12/31	Market adjustment-AFS	340,000	
	Unrealized gain-AFS		340,000
Part b.			
1/1	Investment in stock-X Company	2,100,000	
	Cash		2,100,000
3/12	Cash	43,000	
	Investment in stock-X Company		43,000
12/31	Investment in stock-X Company	46,000	
	Investment income		46,000

Pause and Reflect

The total investment of $2,734,000 is the summation of three different valuation measures. The available-for-sale investments are reported at the fair value of the debt and equity securities in the company's portfolio. The held-to-maturity securities reflect investments at their amortized costs, while the subsidiary investment represents the dollar amount of Supertech's interest in the stockholders' equity of the subsidiary.

Chapter 23
Firm Performance: Profitability

Chapter Overview

The preceding chapters presented the planning and performing phases for the operating, financing, and investing cycles. Chapter 23 is the first chapter on the evaluation phase. This chapter examines firm performance through the lens of profitability. The income statement is an important tool for communicating operating results to external and internal users. Components of income are discussed, and some of these include comprehensive income, discontinued operations, extraordinary items, and cumulative accounting adjustments. The limitations of the income statement are presented also. The statement of retained earnings and statement of owners' equity are illustrated as well. The chapter describes the differences among absorption, unit-variable, and throughput accounting income reports used internally.

This chapter begins a series of chapters dealing with the evaluation phase. It is important for external users and internal users to evaluate the outcomes of the planning and performing phases. In this way, the users can assess their decisions and modify future decisions as necessary. The components of income can provide users with valuable insight about the operations of a business. Become familiar with these components and learn to interpret what this information may reveal about the firm's past and future performance.

Read and Recall Questions

> **Learning Objective:**
> L.O.1. Explain the importance of the components of earnings (income from continuing operations) to users.

According to the FASB's conceptual framework, what are the three objectives of financial reporting?

What is the purpose of the income statement?

What is comprehensive income? What are the elements of comprehensive income?

What are earnings? How do earnings differ from comprehensive income?

What is the difference between a multi-step and single-step format of the income statement?

What does income from continuing operations represent?

Why are notes to the financial statement required?

Learning Objective:
L.O.2. Describe what is important about the components of nonowner changes in equity and cumulative accounting adjustments.

What are discontinued operations? Why are they presented separately on the income statement?

When a segment of a business is discontinued, what two items are reported? Are these items reported before tax or net of tax?

What are extraordinary items? Give two examples of extraordinary items.

Are extraordinary items reported before tax or net of tax?

What are cumulative accounting adjustments? Why are these presented on the income statement? Are they reported before tax or net of tax?

Learning Objective:
L.O.3. Explain the importance of other comprehensive items of income.

According to *SFAS No. 130*, what other items should be included in comprehensive income?

Are other comprehensive income items closed to Retained Earnings? Explain.

Learning Objective:
L.O.4. Explain how companies determine earnings per share and what information it provides to users.

What are earnings per share? Is this the amount stockholders will receive as dividends? Explain.

In its basic form, how are earnings per share calculated?

- Define diluted earnings per share.

Why must companies disclose the per share effect of extraordinary items and accounting changes?

What items must be disclosed for identifiable segments of a company?

Learning Objective:
L.O.5. Identify the elements of the statement of retained earnings.

What is the purpose of the statement of retained earnings? What are the three sources of changes that affect the Retained Earnings account?

What is a prior period adjustment? How is a prior period adjustment reported on the statement of retained earnings?

What information appears on a consolidate statement of stockholders' equity?

What principle leads to inconsistencies in applying the historical cost principle to the reporting of items on the income statement?

How do cost allocations affect reported income?

What is full-absorption costing? What distortions can full-absorption costing introduce into income?

Learning Objective:
L.O.6. Calculate return on investment for business segments.

Identify and describe each of the four types of responsibility centers.

How is each of the responsibility centers evaluated?

What is return on investment? How is return on investment calculated?

Learning Objective:
L.O.7. Describe the differences among absorption, unit-variable, and throughput accounting reports used internally.

Using absorption accounting, how might a manager increase reported earnings?

Describe unit-variable accounting.

Describe throughput accounting.

213
©The McGraw-Hill Companies, Inc., 2000

Why do unit-variable and throughput accounting discourage mangers from overproducing inventory?

Why does throughput accounting produce lower income than absorption or unit-variable accounting?

Learning Objective:
L.O.8. Explain why companies use product line (divisional) income reports.

What are product-line (divisional) income reports?

Why do companies use product-line (divisional) income reports?

Define product margin and segment margin.

Outline of Key Concepts

I. The purpose of the income statement is to reflect the earnings generated by the company during the accounting period.
   A. Income statement information fulfills the FASB's three objectives of financial reporting.
      1. Provides information useful for making investment and credit decisions.
      2. Provides information useful of assessing cash flow prospects.
      3. Provides information relevant to evaluating resources, claims to those resources, and changes in those resources.
   B. Comprehensive income--reflects all changes in owners' equity during the period except those resulting from investments by or distributions to owners and those resulting from the corrections of errors made in prior periods.
      1. The elements of comprehensive income include:
         + Revenues
         - Expenses
         + Gains
         - Losses
         = Earnings (income from continuing operatoins)
         +/- Other nonowner changes in equity
         +/- Cumulative accounting adjustments
         = Net income
         +/- Other comprehensive income items
         = Comprehensive income
      2. Earnings result from business activities that are assumed to be recurring.
      3. Nonowner changes in equity include discontinued operations and extraordinary items.
         a. Discontinued operations are the result of a company selling or disposing of a segment of its business.
         b. Two items are reported about discontinued operations.
            i. Income or loss generated based on the operations of the segment from the beginning of the accounting period through the disposal date (net of tax).
            ii. Gain or loss resulting from the disposal of the segment's net assets (net of tax).
         c. Extraordinary items are events that occurred during the accounting period that are both unusual and infrequent.
            i. Reported net of tax.
            ii. Include assets that are expropriated by a foreign government, losses sustained from a disaster, or material gains and losses from early extinguishment of debt.
      4. Cumulative accounting adjustments are modifications made to the accounting records that result from changes in accounting princples.

a. Occur when a company switches from one generally accepted accounting principle to another.
b. The switch results in a lack of consistency between statements for consecutive reporting periods.
  i. The reason for the inconsistency must be disclosed.
  ii. Cumulative effect is shown because it is not feasible to restate all previous year's financial statements to make them comparable to the current period's statements.
5. *SFAS No. 130* requires that companies report comprehensive income in addition to net income.
  a. Other comprehensive income items include foreign currency translation adjustments, minimum pension liability adjustments, and unrealized gains and losses from certain debt and equity transactions.
    i. Includes the unrealized gains and losses from available-for-sale securities.
  b. Other comprehensive income items appear below net income and are not closed to Retained Earnings at the end of the period.
    i. These items are reported as separate items within the stockholders' equity section of the balance sheet.
C. GAAP requires that companies report segment information based on how management has organized the company.
  1. Must report information about its products, geographic markets, and major customers.

II. Earnings per share (EPS) is a common-size measure of a company's earnings performance that allows the comparison of the operating performance of large and small corporations on a share-for-share basis.
  A. The basic form of earnings per share is calculated as:

  $$\frac{\text{Net Income - Preferred stock dividends}}{\text{Weighted-average number of common shares outstanding}}$$

   1. Preferred dividends are subtracted from net income because preferred stockholders have a first claim on the firm's earnings if any dividends are paid out.
  B. If a company has issued stock options or securities that may be converted to common stock, a diluted earnings per share figure must be disclosed.
   1. It shows the decreased earnings per share that would occur as a result of conversions and the exercise of stock options.

III. Statement of retained earnings indicates the changes that occur in the Retained Earnings account during the period.
  A. The changes arise from three sources.
   1. Net income or loss.
   2. Cash or stock dividends declared.
   3. Prior period adjustments.

    B. A prior period adjustment is a correction of a previously undetected error that affected net income or loss of a previous accounting period.

IV. There are several important issues associated with the income statement.
- A. The income statement has been based on the historical cost assumption.
  1. Conservatism leads a company to anticipate losses but not gains which results in inventory being reported at lower-of-cost-or-market.
     a. The unrealized holding loss is reported in income.
  2. Unrealized gains and losses on trading securities are reported in the income statement.
  3. Results in apparent inconsistencies in the application of historical cost.
- B. Cost allocations do not measure the economic deterioration of assets.
  1. Allocations are methods to allocate the cost of an asset over its expected useful life.
  2. Companies use a variety of cost allocation methods.
  3. Cost allocations are disclosed in the notes to the financial statements.
- C. Full-absorption accounting is required for external reporting on the income statement.
  1. Assigns all production costs such as direct materials, direct labor, unit-variable manufacturing overhead, batch-level overhead, product-sustaining overhead, and facility-sustaining overhead to the units produced.
  2. A company can increase its income simply by increasing the number of units produced during the period, even if the number of units sold remains the same.

V. Internally, income can be reported in different manners to avoid the income manipulation possible with absorption accounting.
- A. Unit-variable accounting--only costs that vary with the number of units produced are included in cost of goods sold.
  1. Batch-level, product-sustaining, and facility-sustaining overhead costs are expensed in total in the period incurred.
- B. Throughput accounting--only direct materials are included in the cost of goods sold.
  1. All other production costs are expensed in total in the period incurred.
  2. Will produce lower income than either absorption or unit-variable accounting.

VI. Internal users require additional reports to evaluate profitability performance.
- A. Evaluations may occur by responsibility center.
  1. Cost center--responsible for controlling costs and providing a good or service in an efficient manner.
     a. Evaluated on costs only.
  2. Revenue center--responsible for generating revenues and promoting the company's products and services effectively.
     a. Evaluated on revenues only.
  3. Profit center--responsible for making a profit; it must effectively generate revenues and efficiently control costs.
     a. Evaluated on profits.

4. Investment center--responsible for using assets in an effective and efficient manner to generate profits.
   a. Evaluated on profits or return on investment.
   b. Return on investment is calculated as:

   $$\frac{\text{Profit of the investment center}}{\text{Assets of the investment center}}$$

B. Product line (divisional) income reports are specific-purpose reports designed to provide more detailed information than general-purpose segment disclosures of the results of operations for a product line or company division.
   1. If the segment is a profit center, segment margins may be adequate for evaluating performance.
   2. If the segment is an investment center, return on investment can be used to evaluate performance.

Problem I

Indicate whether the following statements are either true (T) or false (F).

_____ 1. Comprehensive income only includes those items that are recurring by nature.
_____ 2. Income from discontinued operations will be shown separately on the income statement net of any income tax expense.
_____ 3. Earnings per share is the amount each stockholder received in dividends during the year.
_____ 4. In calculating earnings per share, preferred stock dividends must be subtracted from net income.
_____ 5. The beginning retained earnings balance is adjusted for corrections of previously undetected errors.
_____ 6. Full absorption costing may cause distortions in the income statement due to fixed manufacturing costs that are allocated based on the number of units produced.
_____ 7. Product line income reports are generally less detailed than external income statements.
_____ 8. The purpose of the income statement is to reflect earnings generated by the company during the accounting period.
_____ 9. A change in accounting principles is considered a non-recurring item and would be shown separately on the income statement.
_____ 10. All comprehensive income items are closed to retained earnings.

Problem II

Indicate the correct answer by circling the appropriate letter.

1. During the year, X Corporation had 20,000 shares of $10 par value common stock and 1,000 shares of $100 par value, 10% preferred stock outstanding. X Corporation reported net income of $50,000 for the year. The earnings per share for the year is _____.
   a. $2.00
   b. $2.50
   c. $3.00
   d. $3.50

2. According to the FASB's conceptual framework, which of the following is an objective of financial reporting information?
   a. Provide information useful for making investment and credit decisions
   b. Provide information that is useful for assessing cash flow prospects
   c. Provide information that can be used to evaluate an enterprise's resources, claims to those resources and changes in the resources.
   d. All of the above are objectives of financial reporting.

3. Which of the following would not be included in the computation of earnings (income from continuing operations)?
   a. Revenues
   b. Gains
   c. Losses
   d. Cumulative accounting adjustments

4. Which of the following is not shown net of tax on the income statement?
   a. Extraordinary losses
   b. Cumulative effect of accounting changes
   c. Income from discontinued operations
   d. Gain on sale of equipment

5. Zectar Corporation reported net income of $100,000 for the calendar year 19X4. At the beginning of the year, Zectar had 40,000 shares outstanding. On June 30, 19X4, the company issued 4,000 additional shares of stock. What will the company report as earnings per share for 19X4?
   a. $2.00
   b. $2.50
   c. $2.27
   d. $2.38

©The McGraw-Hill Companies, Inc., 2000

6. Which of the following is an item included in the calculation of comprehensive income but not included in a company's net income?
   a. interest income
   b. gain on the sale of equipment
   c. loss on early retirement of debt
   d. unrealized gain on available-for-sale securities

7. Late in 19X1 it was discovered that Y Corporation failed to accrue $100,000 of vacation pay in 19X0. If Y Corporation's effective tax rate for 19X0 was 40 percent, what adjustment would be made to the beginning retained earnings balance to correct the error?
   a. Increase by $40,000.
   b. Decrease by $60,000.
   c. Decrease by $100,000.
   d. No adjustment is made to retained earnings.

8. Which of the following is an item included in the calculation of comprehensive income but not included in a company's net income?
   a. foreign currency translation adjustments
   b. extraordinary gains and losses
   c. income from discontinued operations
   d. net sales

9. Which of the following would not have to be disclosed for any identifiable segment of a company?
   a. revenues from external customers
   b. depreciation expense of the segment
   c. segment profit or loss
   d. research and development costs of the segment

10. Which of the following would not be included in the statement of changes in retained earnings?
    a. net income or loss
    b. cash or stock dividends declared
    c. prior period adjustments
    d. all of the above are included

11. A _____ center is responsible for both effectively generating revenues and efficiently controlling costs.
    a. cost
    b. revenue
    c. profit
    d. target

12. Which of the following costs will be included in cost of goods sold if the unit-variable accounting method is used?
    a. direct labor cost
    b. batch-related costs
    c. product-sustaining costs
    d. facility-sustaining costs

13. When the throughput accounting method is used, only _____ costs are included in cost of goods sold.
    a. direct labor
    b. direct materials
    c. product-sustaining
    d. facility-sustaining

Problem III

Following is a list of important ideas and key concepts from the chapter. To test your knowledge of these terms, match the term with the definition by placing the number in the space provided.

_____ comprehensive (net) income
_____ cost center
_____ cumulative accounting adjustments
_____ diluted earnings per share
_____ discontinued operations
_____ earnings
_____ earnings per share
_____ extraordinary items
_____ investment center
_____ prior period adjustment
_____ product line (divisional) income report
_____ profit center
_____ revenue center
_____ throughput accounting
_____ unit-variable accounting

1. Earnings per share that reflect the amount of decrease in earnings per share that would occur as a result of activities like conversions and the exercise of stock options

2. A center that is responsible for using assets in an effective and efficient manner to generate profits

3. Modifications made to the accounting records that result from changes in accounting principles which occur when a company switches from one generally accepted method of accounting to another or when a company adopts a new accounting principle

4. A center that is responsible for making a profit; it must effectively generate revenues and efficiently control costs

5. A center that is responsible for controlling costs and providing a good or service in an efficient manner

6. Specific purpose internal reports designed to provide more detailed information than general purpose income statements regarding the results of operations for a product line or company division

7. A method of determining profits in which only costs that vary with the number of units produced are included in cost of goods sold a batch-related, product-sustaining, and facility-sustaining overhead costs are expensed as incurred

8. Income that reflects all changes in owners' equity during the period except those resulting from investments by, or distributions to, owners and those resulting from errors made in previous periods

9. A common-size measure of a company's earnings performance; the reported net income of the company less preferred dividends for the period divided by the weighted-average number of common shares outstanding

10. Income from continuing operations. Includes revenues minus expenses plus gains minus losses

11. A method of determining profits in which only direct materials are included in cost of goods sold and all other production costs are expensed as incurred

12. Events that occurred during the accounting period that are *both* unusual and infrequent

13. A center that is responsible for generating revenues and promoting the company's products and services effectively

14. A correction of a previously undetected error that affected the net income or loss from a previous accounting period

15. The result of a company selling or disposing of a segment of its business

Problem IV

The following account balances were reported by Ace Company for the accounting year:

Cost of goods sold	$240,000	Income from discontinued operations	$60,000
Interest income	5,000	Gain on sale of equipment	8,000
Flood loss	100,000	Net sales	800,000
Selling expenses	75,000	Interest expense	12,000
General and administrative expense	213,000		

The flood loss is considered both unusual and infrequent. Ace Company's effective tax rate is 40 percent.

1. Prepare a multi-step income statement for the accounting period.

Problem IV (continued)

2. Prepare a single-step income statement for the accounting period.

Problem V

Complete the following sentences by filling in the correct response.

1. The purpose of the income statement is to reflect the _____ generated by the company during the _____ period.

2. Comprehensive income reflects both _____ and _____ aspects of the firm's _____.

3. Earnings include those items that are _____ by nature.

4. Extraordinary items are events that are both _____ and _____.

5. Earnings per share is the _____ _____ available to _____ shareholders, divided by the _____ number of shares outstanding.

6. The _____ statement is the most widely quoted of the financial statements.

Pause and Reflect

OverNite Delivery Company is an air express package delivery company. On a recent flight between Atlanta, Georgia, and Kansas City, Missouri, the airplane crashed into a warehouse owned by Weber Mfg. Company in Joplin, Missouri. Fortunately, no lives were lost. However, OverNite incurred uninsured losses of $1.5 million and Weber suffered $300,000 in uninsured losses. Would either of these losses be classified as an extraordinary item? Why or why not?

_____
_____
_____
_____
_____
_____
_____
_____

©The McGraw-Hill Companies, Inc., 2000

Solutions for Chapter 23

Problem I

1. F
2. T
3. F
4. T
5. T
6. T
7. F
8. T
9. T
10. F

Problem II

1. a
2. d
3. d
4. d
5. d
6. d
7. b
8. a
9. d
10. d
11. c
12. a
13. b

Problem III

- 8   comprehensive (net) income
- 5   cost center
- 3   cumulative accounting adjustments
- 1   diluted earnings per share
- 15   discontinued operations
- 10   earnings
- 9   earnings per share
- 12   extraordinary items

- 2   investment center
- 14   prior period adjustment
- 6   product line (divisional) income report
- 4   profit center
- 13   revenue center
- 11   throughput accounting
- 7   unit-variable accounting

Problem IV

1.

Ace Company
Income Statement

Net sales		$800,000
Less cost of goods sold		240,000
Gross margin		$560,000
Operating expenses:		
Selling expenses	$ 75,000	
General and administrative expenses	213,000	288,000
Income from operations		$272,000
Other revenues/<expenses>:		
Interest expense	<12,000>	
Interest income	5,000	
Gain on sale of equipment	8,000	1,000
Income from continuing operations before taxes		$273,000
Income tax expense		109,200
Income from continuing operations		$163,800
Discontinued operations:		
Income from discontinued division, net of taxes		36,000
Income before extraordinary items		$199,800
Extraordinary loss from flood, net of taxes		60,000
Net Income		$139,800

Problem IV (continued)

2.

Ace Company
Income Statement

Revenues:		
Net sales	$800,000	
Interest income	5,000	
Gain on sale of equipment	8,000	
		$813,000
Costs and expenses:		
Less cost of goods sold	$240,000	
Selling expenses	75,000	
General and administrative expenses	213,000	
Interest expense	12,000	
Income tax expense	109,200	
		$649,200
Income from continuing operations		$163,800
Discontinued operations:		
Income from discontinued division, net of taxes		36,000
Income before extraordinary items		$199,800
Extraordinary loss from flood, net of taxes		60,000
Net Income		$139,800

Problem V

1. earnings, accounting
2. recurring, non-recurring, earnings
3. recurring
4. unusual, infrequent
5. net income, common, weighted-average
6. income

Pause and Reflect

An extraordinary item must be both unusual and infrequent in occurrence. Based upon this definition, OverNite Delivery Company would not classify its loss as extraordinary. Although the plane crash would be infrequent in occurrence, it is not unusual for airplanes to crash. Weber Mfg. Co. could classify its loss as extraordinary. The fact that Weber's warehouse was destroyed by a plane crashing into it is both unusual and infrequent in occurrence.

Chapter 24
Firm Performance: Financial Position

Chapter Overview

Chapter 24 continues the examination of the evaluation phase. It explores the statement of financial position, more commonly known as the balance sheet. The balance sheet presents a company's assets and claims to those assets by owners and creditors. The classification of assets, liabilities, and owners' equity allows readers of the balance sheet to assess the significance of each category. Proper classification of balance sheet items helps the users assess some of the uses of future profits and cash flows. In addition, a user can use balance sheet information to assess the liquidity and solvency of a firm.

By examining a company's financial position, a user has another perspective for evaluating the results of a firm's operations. It is important that you learn to classify asset, liability, and owners' equity accounts correctly. These classifications have important implications for a user's ability to assess profits and cash flows. You should attempt to link the evaluation of financial position with the previous chapter's evaluation of profitability.

Read and Recall Questions

> **Learning Objective:**
> L.O.1. Understand the implications of classifying assets and liabilities as short term or long term.

What information does financial position convey?

How does financial position reveal future profit potential?

Define liquidity. Define solvency.

Define current assets. What is the operating cycle?

Define current liabilities.

How would the reclassification of a liability from current to long term affect how investors and creditors perceive liquidity and solvency?

How does the proper classification of current items affect the current and quick ratios?

Learning Objective:
L.O.2. Describe the proper classification of assets, liabilities, and equity items on the balance sheet.

In what order are assets listed on the balance sheet?

What assets are included within the current asset classification?

What is a compensating balance? How would it be classified?

What items would be included in marketable securities?

At what amount are accounts receivable reported on the balance sheet?

What information about accounts and notes receivable should appear in the notes to the financial statements?

At what amount should inventories be reported on the balance sheet?

What information is included in the section of an annual report called summary of significant accounting policies?

Why are prepaid expenses classified as current assets?

What is included in the investments section of the balance sheet?

What items are included in property, plant, and equipment?

Why do capital leases appear on the balance sheet?

How are natural resources reported on the balance sheet?

At what amount are intangible assets reported on the balance sheet?

What items may be found in the other assets section of the balance sheet?

What are deferred charges?

What four events create current liabilities?

What are long-term liabilities? Is it possible for a liability that will be paid in the coming fiscal period to be classified as long term? Explain.

How do bonds payable differ from long-term notes payable?

What type of information about a bond issue may be presented in the notes to the financial statements?

What types of obligations would be classified as other long-term liabilities?

What is off-balance sheet financing? How might off-balance sheet financing affect an investor's or creditor's perception of a company's financial position?

Why is stockholders' equity divided into contributed capital and retained earnings?

What items appear in contributed capital?

What is included in valuation capital? Where does it appear on the balance sheet?

Why may corporations restrict retained earnings?

How is treasury stock reported on the balance sheet?

Learning Objective:
L.O.3. Describe some of the additional financial disclosures beyond the financial statements themselves.

How does management convey its view in the annual report?

What type of information must be included in business segment disclosures? What is the threshold for disclosure?

Why do companies issue quarterly financial statements?

What are contingent liabilities? How are they disclosed?

What is the purpose of the auditor's report?

Briefly describe each of the four kinds of reports issued by external auditors.

Why may current cost valuations be used for internal reporting?

Why does GAAP use historical cost rather than current cost valuations for financial reporting?

Outline of Key Concepts

I. Financial position conveys information about the nature of the company's resources and obligations, its ability to meet its obligations, and its prospects for future profitability.
   A. Balance sheet (statement of financial position)--reports the amount and type of assets the firm controls and the claims the owners and creditors have on those assets on the last day of the reporting period.
   B. Classifying assets and liabilities as current and noncurrent helps creditors and others assess the company's short-term liquidity and solvency.
      1. Liquidity--time required for a firm to convert its assets to cash.
      2. Solvency--ability to meet obligations when they are due.
      3. Decision to classify assets and liabilities as long term or short term is often subjective.
      4. Management realizes that reporting more assets as current and classifying liabilities as long term rather than short term enhances the appearance of a firm's liquidity.

II. Balance sheet classifications provide additional information.
   A. Asset classifications are listed in order of their liquidity, which is how quickly the firm will convert them to cash or consume them as part of operations.
      1. Current assets are listed in order of liquidity also.
         a. Cash is reported at its stated value.
            i. Includes petty cash funds
            ii. Does not include compensating balances--minimum cash balance that the depositor must maintain to either continue to earn interest on the amount deposited in the bank account or to avoid certain fees from the bank.
         b. Marketable securities are temporary investments that companies intend to convert to cash when needed.
            i. Reported at their market value.
         c. Account receivables are reported at their net realizable value.
            i. Notes to the balance sheet would disclose the amount of the allowance for doubtful accounts, provisions for discounts and allowances, and foreign currency exchange rate fluctuations.
         d. Inventory--company must disclose the inventory method and whether it reports the inventory amount at the lower of its cost or market value at the end of the period.
         e. Prepaid expenses--support the operating activities of the firm and are usually consumed during the operating cycle.
      2. Investment classification describes the type and extent of the company's long-term, nonoperational investments.
         a. Footnotes provide detailed descriptions of a company's investments.
      3. Property, plant, and equipment reports the tangible operational investments that support the infrastructure of the firm.

    a. Depreciable assets are shown at their book value.
    b. Includes capital leases and natural resources.
  4. Intangible assets, which have no physical substance but generate future economic benefits, are reported at their original cost less amortization taken to date.
  5. Other assets are items that do not fit in other asset classifications.
    a. Includes items like noncurrent receivables, special funds, and deferred charges.
       i. Deferred charges--long-term prepayments that companies amortize over the period management believes the firm will benefit from the expenditures. An example is organization costs.
B. Liabilities are debts and other obligations.
  1. Current liabilities are listed first and result from:
    a. The receipt of loan proceeds by the firm.
    b. The receipt of goods and services when using credit as a means of payment.
    c. The receipt of prepayments for goods and services promised to be provided by the firm during the next year.
    d. Includes the reclassification of the portion of long-term debt that becomes due within the coming fiscal year.
       i. Remains long-term if the debt will be repaid with long-term assets or will be refinanced.
  2. Long-term liabilities are not expected to come due within one year or the operating cycle, whichever is longer.
    a. Terms and features of the long-term debt agreements are disclosed in the notes to the financial statements.
    b. Other long-term liabilities include such items as pension obligations, capital lease obligations, and deferred income tax liabilities.
       i. Deferred income tax liabilities (or assets) arise from the differences between computing income using generally accepted accounting principles and computing taxable income using tax law.
  3. Understanding the nature of liability classifications helps the financial statement reader assess the nature of the firm's obligations.
C. Stockholders' equity is divided among contributed capital, donated capital, valuation capital, and retained earnings.
  1. Contributed capital reflects the amounts invested in the company by the stockholders.
    a. Preferred and common stock are reported separately.
    b. Notes to the financial statements disclose information about number of shares outstanding, stock splits or dividends, preferred stock liquidation values, and treasury stock transactions.
  2. Donated capital is used when a corporation receives an asset but gives no ownership interest (stock) in exchange.
    a. A donated asset is recorded at its fair market value.
  3. Valuation capital most frequently arises from fluctuations in the market value of investments classified as available-for-sale securities.

4. Retained earnings represent the earnings that have not been distributed to the stockholders.
   a. Restrictions may limit the dividend-paying ability of the corporation.
5. Treasury stock is a temporary reduction in the total amount of stockholders' equity.

III. Annual reports contain many types of required and voluntary disclosures.
   A. Management letter to stockholders--gives an overview of the items in the annual report and highlights important aspects of the company's financial performance.
   B. Business segment information must be presented anytime a segment accounts for 10 percent or more of total company sales or assets.
      1. A segment can be an identifiable geographic region or an identifiable product line.
      2. Such information helps investors assess the prospects of future sales and earnings associated with specific business segments.
   C. Contingent liabilities represent events that could create negative financial results for company at some future point.
      1. Must disclose the existence of the contingent liabilities in the notes even when the corporation cannot estimate the impact of the events or whether the likelihood of such events is less than probable.
      2. An actual loss must be recorded when the event is considered probable and when the company can estimate its monetary effect on the financial statements.
   D. Auditor's report discloses the CPA's opinion about the fairness of the financial statements using GAAP as the criteria.
      1. Unqualified opinion--financial statements are fair representations of the business's financial position and reported income and that, in the auditor's opinion, the company has applied GAAP appropriately.
      2. Qualified opinion--either the auditors found parts of the company's financial statements are not in accordance with GAAP, or that the auditor's ability to examine the underlying records used to develop the financial statements was limited.
      3. Adverse opinion--the external auditor believes the financial statements are not fair representations of the company's financial position or income.
      4. Disclaimer of opinion--the auditor was not able to gather sufficient evidence to support an opinion or the auditor was not sufficiently independent of the company to issue an opinion.

IV. Balance sheets prepared for internal use may use a current cost valuation rather than historical cost.
   A. Current cost information has two problems.
      1. Obtaining current cost information may be costly.
      2. Current cost information may be subjective.

Problem I

Indicate whether the following statements are either true (T) or false (F).

_____1. Management's classification of current and noncurrent assets and liabilities may be subjective.
_____2. Financial position is used to communicate the future profit potential of a company.
_____3. Restricting retained earnings will limit the dividend-paying ability of a company.
_____4. Internal management reports must following GAAP reporting requirements.
_____5. Classifying assets and liabilities into current and noncurrent helps in the assessment of a company's short-term liquidity.
_____6. A qualified opinion means that all elements in the financial statements are prepared in accordance with GAAP.
_____7. A liability that is due in six months and that will be refinanced with a twenty-year bond, will be classified as a current liability.
_____8. Bonds are always carried on the balance sheet at their face value.
_____9. Deferred tax liabilities (assets) are generated due to differences between the computation of financial reporting income and taxable income.
_____10. Treasury stock is added to other contributed capital in the stockholders' equity section of the balance sheet.
_____11. An audit report is based on the testing of every transaction entered into by the company under examination.

Problem II

1. Classifying assets and liabilities as current and noncurrent helps to answer questions about a company's _____.
    a. short-term liquidity
    b. asset utilization
    c. short-term profitability
    d. long-term profitability

2. An asset will generally be classified as current if it will be converted to cash or used in operations within _____ of the balance sheet date.
    a. 6 months
    b. one year
    c. 18 months
    d. 2 years

3. Which of the following would not be considered a current liability?
    a. accounts payable due in 60 days
    b. note payable due in 9 months
    c. interest payable due in 3 months
    d. bond payable maturing in 2 months that will be refinanced with a twenty-year bond

4. Inventory will be carried on the balance sheet at _____.
    a. cost
    b. market value
    c. lower of cost or market
    d. its sales price

5. Buildings will be carried on the balance sheet at _____.
    a. cost
    b. market value
    c. replacement value
    d. book value

6. Which of the following would not be considered an asset of a company?
    a. cash
    b. patent
    c. lease obligation
    d. copyright

7. Which of the following would not be shown in the stockholders' equity section of the balance sheet?
    a. retained earnings
    b. donated capital
    c. treasury stock
    d. marketable securities

8. A contingent liability must be reported on the balance sheet if the following condition(s) is/are met.
    a. the event is considered probable
    b. the company can estimate the monetary effect
    c. it is possible the company will have to pay
    d. both (a) and (b) must be met

9. A(n) _____ opinion indicates that either the auditor found parts of the company's financial statements not in accordance with GAAPP or the auditor's ability to examine the underlying records used to develop the financial statements was limited.
   a. unqualified
   b. qualified
   c. adverse
   d. disclaimed

10. Which of the following would not be considered a current asset.
    a. inventory
    b. accounts receivable
    c. equipment
    d. prepaid rent

Problem III

Following is a list of important ideas and key concepts from the chapter. To test your knowledge of these terms, match the term with the definition by placing the number in the space provided.

_____ adverse opinion　　　　　　　　_____ off-balance sheet financing
_____ compensating balance　　　　　_____ qualified opinion
_____ contingent liabilities　　　　　　_____ segment data
_____ deferred charges (deferrals)　　_____ summary of significant
_____ disclaimer of opinion　　　　　　　　　　accounting policies
_____ letter to stockholders　　　　　_____ unqualified opinion

1. The report issued by independent auditors stating that the financial statements are fair representations of the business's financial position and reported income and that the company has applied GAAP appropriately.

2. A minimum cash balance that the depositor (company) must maintain either to continue to earn interest on the amount deposited in the bank account or to avoid certain fees, such as service charges.

3. Long-term prepayments frequently found in the "other assets" classification that companies amortize over various lengths of time, depending on how long the company will benefit from the expenditures.

4. Borrowing money in ways that would avoid having to record the obligation on the balance sheet.

5. Part of the annual report that discloses financial information for product lines or identifiable geographic regions that account for ten percent or more of total sales or assets.

6. Management's written report that presents an overview of the items in the annual report other than financial statements and highlights important aspects of financial performance.

7. Events that could create negative financial results for a company; required to be recorded when the event is probable *and* estimable in terms of its monetary effects.

8. The report issued by the external auditor that indicates that the financial statements are not fair representations of the company's financial position or income.

9. The report issued by independent auditors stating that parts of the financial statements are not in accordance with GAAP or that the auditor's ability to examine the underlying records used to develop the financial statements was limited.

10. Part of accompanying notes to the financial statements that describe the accounting principles and methods the company has chosen to use.

11. The report issued by an external auditor that indicates that the auditor was not able to gather sufficient evidence to support an opinion or that the auditor was not sufficiently independent of the company to issue an opinion.

Problem IV

Complete the following sentences by filling in the correct response.

1. The _____ _____ reports the amount and type of assets the firm controls and the _____ the owners and creditors have on those assets.

2. Segments can by identified on _____ region or _____ line basis.

3. Financial position is measured at a _____ in time whereas net income is measured for a _____ of time.

4. Intangible assets have no _____ substance, but are expected to generate some future _____ benefit.

5. Any time that a segment accounts for _____ percent or more of total company sales or _____, related segment data must appear as part of the _____ report.

6. Contingent liabilities must be recorded in the financial statements if the event is considered _____ and the amount can be reasonably _____.

Problem V

The following account balances are available for the Sunflex Company as of December 31, 19X7.

Sales	900,000	Accounts receivable	89,000
Bonds payable	600,000	Capital stock	500,000
Cost of goods sold	500,000	Inventory	165,000
Equipment	700,000	Accumulated depreciation	145,000
Patents	75,000	Selling expenses	85,000
Short-term notes payable	40,000	Interest expense	70,000
Premium on bonds payable	143,000	Land	245,000
General and admin. expenses	210,000	Accounts payable	61,000
Treasury stock	19,000	Retained earnings (beginning of year)	184,000
Cash	62,000	Allow. for uncollectible accounts	6,000
Prepaid insurance	8,000	Marketable securities (trading)	23,000
Salaries payable	17,000	Investment in stock - X Company	345,000

Required: Prepare a classified balance sheet.

Problem VI

Using the following legend, indicate the proper balance sheet classification for each account:

CA	Current assets	NL	Noncurrent liabilities
PPE	Property, plant, and equipment	CC	Contributed capital
INT	Intangibles	RE	Retained earnings
ONA	Other noncurrent assets	OOE	Other owners' equity
CL	Current liabilities		

_____ 1. Cash
_____ 2. Salaries payable
_____ 3. Prepaid rent
_____ 4. Mortgage payable
_____ 5. Preferred stock
_____ 6. Land
_____ 7. Retained earnings
_____ 8. Equipment
_____ 9. Common stock
_____ 10. Unearned service revenue
_____ 11. Accounts receivable
_____ 12. Goodwill
_____ 13. Accounts payable
_____ 14. Copyrights
_____ 15. Bonds payable
_____ 16. Notes payable (due in 6 months)
_____ 17. Treasury stock
_____ 18. Paid-in-capital common stock
_____ 19. Inventory
_____ 20. Supplies

Pause and Reflect

Jeff and Steve recently began investing money in corporate stocks. One evening while evaluating a company's annual report, they read the auditor's opinion. It was an unqualified opinion, which stated that the financial statements presented fairly the financial position, results of operations, and cash flows in conformity with generally accepted accounting principles. Steve believes the opinion means the financial statements are free of errors and any fraudulent misrepresentations. Jeff disagrees. He asserts that there is no way an auditor could detect every error or fraudulent act that occurs in a big corporation. Who is right and why?

Solutions for Chapter 24

Problem I

1. T
2. T
3. T
4. F
5. T
6. F
7. F
8. F
9. T
10. F
11. F

Problem II

1. a
2. b
3. d
4. c
5. d
6. c
7. d
8. d
9. b
10. c

Problem III

8   adverse opinion
2   compensating balance
7   contingent liabilities
3   deferred charges (deferrals)
11 disclaimer of opinion
6   letter to stockholders
4   off-balance sheet financing
9   qualified opinion
5   segment data
10 summary of significant accounting policies
1   unqualified opinion

Problem IV

1. balance sheet, claims
2. geographical, product
3. point, period
4. physical, economic
5. ten, assets, annual
6. probable, estimated

Problem V

Current Assets:
Cash		$ 62,000
Marketable securities		23,000
Accounts receivable	89,000	
Less: Allowance for uncollectible accounts	6,000	83,000
Inventory		165,000
Prepaid insurance		8,000
Total current assets		341,000

Property, Plant and Equipment:
Land		245,000
Equipment	700,000	
Less: Accumulated depreciation	145,000	555,000
Total property, plant and equipment		800,000

Intangible Assets - Patents	75,000
Other Assets - Investment in stock - X Company	345,000
Total Assets	**$1,561,000**

Liabilities and Stockholders' Equity

Current Liabilities:
Accounts payable		$ 61,000
Notes payable		40,000
Salaries payable		17,000
Total current liabilities		118,000

Non-current Liabilities:
Bonds payable	600,000	
Add: Premium on bonds payable	143,000	743,000

Stockholders' Equity:
Capital stock	500,000
Retained earnings	219,000
	719,000
Less: Treasury stock	19,000
Total stockholders' equity	700,000
Total Liabilities and Stockholders' Equity	**$1,561,000**

Problem VI

1. CA
2. CL
3. CA
4. NL
5. CC
6. PPE
7. RE
8. PPE
9. CC
10. CL
11. CA
12. INT
13. CL
14. INT
15. NL
16. CL
17. OOE
18. CC
19. CA
20. CA

Pause and Reflect

Jeff is correct. Auditors perform their audit examinations on a test basis, which means there is no audit or verification of every transaction. Auditors do attempt to gather sufficient information to support their opinion that the statements are materially correct, but they do not attempt to correct every error because they rely upon the principle of materiality. In addition, auditors do not assert that the statements are right; they state that the financial statements make a fair presentation in accordance with generally accepted accounting principles. Therefore, it is quite possible that errors and minor fraudulent activities were not discovered.

Chapter 25
Firm Performance: Cash Flows

Chapter Overview

Chapter 25 examines the statement of cash flows. The chapter presents both the direct and indirect methods for preparing the statement. The purpose of the statement of cash flows is to illustrate the cash flows arising from the operating, investing, and financing activities of a firm. The chapter discusses how external and internal users can use the cash flow information to assess a firm's ability to generate positive future cash flows and meet its obligations.

The FASB recommends that the direct method be used to present the statement of cash flows and that a reconciliation of net income and cash flows be provided as supplemental information. This reconciliation takes the form of an indirect method statement of cash flows. As a result, many companies present only statements using the indirect method. Your instructor may ask you to learn both approaches, or he or she may prefer that you focus your attention on one method.

Read and Recall Questions

> **Learning Objective:**
> L.O.1. Describe the information companies provide users through the statement of cash flows.

What are the four primary purposes of the statement of cash flows?

Why is the statement of cash flows divided into three sections?

What types of cash flows are included in the operating activities section?

How may the reader of the statement of cash flows use the cash flow information contained in the operating activities section?

What type of information is contained in the investing activities section of the statement of cash flows? How may readers of the statement use this information?

What type of information is contained in the financing activities section of the statement of cash flows? How may readers of the statement use this information?

How do the direct and indirect formats of the statement of cash flows differ? What are the advantages and disadvantages of each format?

What is the relationship of the statement of cash flows to the balance sheet, income statement, and statement of retained earnings?

Learning Objective:
L.O.2. Discuss how companies determine and analyze cash flows from operating activities using the direct format.

Using the direct format, briefly explain how to determine the cash flows for a particular operating item on income statement.

Why do a company's revenues shown on the income statement differ from its cash inflows from operations?

How is the amount of cash receipts from customers calculated?

How is the amount of cash received from prepaid customers calculated?

Why do a company's expenses differ from the amounts of cash paid for expense items?

How is the amount of cash paid for prepaid expenses calculated?

How is the amount of cash paid for accrued expenses calculated?

How is the amount of cash paid for interest calculated?

- How is the amount of cash paid for inventory determined?

How can users of the statement of cash flows determine if a company is collecting revenues and paying current obligations in a timely fashion?

> **Learning Objective:**
> L.O.3. Discuss how companies determine and analyze cash flows from operating activities using the indirect format.

- What are the four adjustments that must be made to convert net income to cash from operations?

Explain how noncash income statement items must be adjusted to convert net income to cash from operations. What are two common noncash adjustments?

Why must net income be adjusted for gains and losses when converting it to cash flows from operations?

What are noncash current operating assets? What does an increase in a noncash current asset indicate?

Would a decrease in a noncash operating asset related to revenues be added to or subtracted from net income to determine cash flows from operations? Explain.

Would a decrease in a noncash current operating asset related to expenses be added to or deducted from net income to determine cash flows from operations? Explain.

What are current operating liabilities? What does an increase in a current operating liability indicate?

When a current operating liability related to revenues increases, would the increase be added to or subtracted from net income to determine cash flows from operations? Explain.

When a current operating liability related to expenses increases, would the increase be added to or subtracted from net income to determine cash flows from operations? Explain.

When a company uses the indirect format, what two additional disclosures must be made either on the statement of cash flows itself or in the accompanying notes?

How could the reader of a statement of cash flows prepared in the indirect format use the ratio of cash flows from operations to net income?

Learning Objective:
L.O.4. Explain how companies determine and analyze cash flows from investing activities.

What do the cash flows from the investing activities section reflect?

How would the cash flows associated with trading securities be determined?

How would the cash flows associated with buildings be determined?

Why do financial statement users evaluate investing cash flows?

Learning Objective:
L.O.5. Discuss how companies determine and analyze cash flows from financing activities.

What are cash flows from financing activities associated with?

How would cash flows associated with notes payable be determined?

How would cash flows associated with treasury stock be determined?

How would cash flows associated with dividends be determined?

Why do financial statement users evaluate financing cash flows?

Why are significant noncash investing and financing events reported either on the statement of cash flows itself or in the notes to the financial statements?

Outline of Key Concepts

I. Statement of cash flows provides the link between accrual-based income statement and the balance sheet.
   A. FASB identified four primary purposes for the statement.
      1. Assess the entity's ability to generate positive future net cash flows.
      2. Assess the entity's ability to meet its obligations and pay dividends, and its need for external financing.
      3. Assess the reasons for differences between income and associated cash receipts and payments.
      4. Assess both the cash and noncash aspects of the entity's investing and financing transactions during the period.
   B. The statement is divided into three major sections.
      1. Operating activities involve transactions that result from the earnings process of the company.
         a. Cash inflows are primarily from customers and interest and dividends received by the company.
         b. Cash outflows result from the payments made for operating expenses, including the purchase of inventory.
         c. This section allows readers to assess the following.
            i. The entity's ability to generate positive future cash flows.
            ii. Assess the differences between accounting income and associated cash receipts and payments.
      2. Investing activities involve acquiring and disposing of property, plant, and equipment; other long-term investments; and short-term or temporary investments that are not cash equivalents.
         a. Allows the reader of the statement to assess the entity's ability to continue to operate and pay dividends as well as its need for external financing.
      3. Financing activities involve borrowing from and repaying creditors, raising funds from owners, and distributing funds to owners that are either a return on or a return of investment.
         a. Allows the reader of the statement to assess the entity's ability to pay dividends as well as its ability to invest in additional assets.

II. The direct format of the statement of cash flows shows the actual cash inflows and outflows from operating activities.
   A. Indicates the amounts of cash received from customers and other sources of cash such as dividends and interest.
      1. Shows how much cash was paid for interest, taxes, and other operating activities.
      2. FASB requires a reconciliation of accrual-based net income to the amount of cash flows from operating activities.

B. To determine the cash flows for particular item, companies use the beginning and ending balances of a given balance sheet account, along with the related revenue or expense amount from the income statement.
 1. Revenues might differ from cash inflows for two reasons.
    a. The revenue is earned before the cash is collected.
        Beginning balance of Accounts Receivable, net
      + Sales on account during the period
      = Maximum amount of cash owed by customers
      - Uncollectible accounts expense
      - Sales discounts
      - Sales returns and allowances
      - Sales returns and allowance
      - **Cash collected from customers**
      = Ending balance of Accounts Receivable, net
    b. The cash is collected before the revenue is earned.
        Beginning balance of revenue collected in advance
      + **Cash received from customers during the period**
      = Maximum goods or services owed to customers
      - Revenues earned during the period
      = Ending balance of revenue collected in advance
 2. Expenses may not equal cash paid for two reasons.
    a. The expenses are incurred before the cash is paid.
        Beginning balance of prepaid asset
      + **Cash paid for prepaid asset**
      = Maximum prepaid asset available
      - Expense during the period
      = Ending balance of prepaid asset
    b. The expenses are incurred after the cash is paid.
        Beginning balance of accrued liability
      + Expense for the period
      = Maximum amount of cash owed
      - **Cash paid during the period**
      = Ending balance of accrued liability
 3. Determining the amount of cash paid for inventory.
        Beginning balance of inventory
      + Purchases during the period
      = Maximum amount of inventory available for sale
      - Purchases returns and allowances
      - Cost of goods sold
      = Ending balance of inventory

          Beginning balance of Accounts Payable
+ Purchases during the period
= Maximum amount of cash owed for inventory
− Purchase returns and allowances
− **Cash paid for inventory during the period**
= Ending balance of Accounts Payable

    4. Although the exact timing of cash flows is unknown to external users, they can use ratios to get a general idea of the timing by examining two ratios.
       a. Percentage of amount due from customers collected during the period.

$$\frac{\text{Cash collected from customers}}{\text{Beginning accounts receivable} + \text{Sales}}$$

       b. Percentage of amount owed to suppliers paid during the period.

$$\frac{\text{Cash paid to inventory suppliers}}{\text{Beginning accounts payable} + \text{Purchases}}$$

III. Indirect format shows the differences between accrual-based net income and cash flows from operating activities.
   A. Over 95 percent of companies use this approach.
   B. Four adjustments to net income are required to determine cash flows from operating activities.
     1. Adjustments for noncash income statement items that increase or decrease income but do not affect operating cash flows.
       a. Depreciation, amortization, and depletion are added back to net income.
       b. Interest expense adjustments due to premiums or discounts are deducted from or added to net income.
       c. Interest income adjustments due to premiums or discounts are added to or deducted from net income.
     2. Adjustments for gains and losses from either investing or financing activities.
       a. Gains must be subtracted from net income.
       b. Losses must be added to net income.
     3. Adjustments for changes in noncash current operating assets must be added to or deducted from net income.

Change in Account	Adjustment to Net Income
Increase in current asset	Subtract amount of increase
Decrease in current asset	Add amount of decrease

     4. Adjustments for changes in current operating liabilities must be added to or deducted from net income.

Change in Account	Adjustment to Net Income
Increase in current liability	Add amount of increase
Decrease in current liability	Subtract amount of decrease

   C. Difficult for external users to analyze cash inflows and outflows with the indirect format.

1. Ratio of cash flows from operations to net income may be compared with other companies in the same industry.
    a. Cash flows from operations/Net income

IV. Determination and analysis of cash flows from investing activities.
   A. The cash flows in this section reflect the amount of cash received from sales of long-term and current nonoperating assets and the amount of cash paid to purchase these assets.
      1. Users evaluate investing cash flows to determine if a company is making adequate investments in long-term assets and other investments.
      2. Investing cash flows may be compared over time and against other companies in the industry.

V. Determination and analysis of cash flows from financing activities.
   A. These cash flows are associated with long-term liabilities, current nonoperating liabilities such as nontrade notes payable and dividends payable, and owners' equity of the company.
      1. Includes the issuance and repayment of notes and bonds, the sale and repurchase of stock, and the distribution of the company's earnings.
      2. Users evaluate financing cash flows to determine if the company is obtaining adequate amounts of cash to enable it to invest in long-term assets.
      3. Financing cash flows may be compared over time and against other companies in the industry.

VI. Noncash investing and financing activities that are important to the financial statement readers are reported either on the statement itself or in the notes to the financial statements.
   A. Typical noncash events reported include.
      1. Acquisition of assets by issuing debt or equity securities.
      2. Exchanges of assets.
      3. Conversion of debt or preferred stock to common stock.
      4. Issuance of common or preferred stock to retire debt.
   B. These events are important because of their future cash flow implications.

Problem I

Indicate whether the following statements are either true (T) or false (F).

____ 1. Net cash flows from operating activities will be the same under both the direct and indirect format.
____ 2. The sale of equipment will be shown in the financing activities section of the cash flow statement.
____ 3. The issuance of common stock will be shown in the investing activities section of the cash flow statement.
____ 4. A company's revenues on the income statement will generally equal its cash receipts from operations.
____ 5. Interest expense paid on a bond payable will be shown in the operating activities section of the cash flow statement.
____ 6. The payment of a cash dividend will be shown in the financing activities section of the cash flow statement.
____ 7. The cash flow statement is used to assess both the cash and noncash aspects of the entity's investing and financing transactions during the period.
____ 8. Most company's use the direct method to report cash flows from operating activities.
____ 9. The issuance of a bond payable will be shown in the investing activities section of the cash flow statement.
____ 10. Cash collected from customers will be shown in the operating activities section of the cash flow statement.

Problem II

Indicate the correct answer by circling the appropriate letter.

1. During the year X Corporation reported salary expense of $235,000 in its income statement. Salaries payable had a beginning balance of $28,000 and an ending balance of $21,000. Cash paid for wages during the year was _____.
   a. $235,000
   b. $242,000
   c. $228,000
   d. $258,000

2. Z Corporation reported interest income of $32,000 for the year. The interest receivable account had a beginning balance of $14,000 and an ending balance of $2,000. What was the cash received from interest for the year?
   a. $34,000
   b. $32,000
   c. $44,000
   d. $20,000

3. Y Corporation reported insurance expense of $12,000 for the most recent accounting period. At the beginning of the period the prepaid insurance account had a $2,400 balance and at the end of the period it had a balance of $1,200. Cash paid for insurance for the accounting period was _____.
   a. $12,000
   b. $13,200
   c. $10,800
   d. $14,400

4. The following selected information is available for the year:
Net income	$500,000
Depreciation expense	34,000
Loss on early retirement of bonds	5,000
Decrease in inventory	12,000
Increase in supplies	2,000
Amortization expense-patent	9,000

   What is the company's net cash flow from operations?
   a. $516,000
   b. $456,000
   c. $504,000
   d. $558,000

Use the following information for the next three questions:

Following are selected account balances for the Suntime Company:

Sales (all on credit)	$450,000
Cost of goods sold	245,000
Supplies expense	9,000

	Beginning balance	Ending balance
Accounts receivable	$85,000	$73,000
Inventory	68,000	93,000
Supplies	1,200	1,500
Accounts payable (inventory purchases)	38,000	25,000

©The McGraw-Hill Companies, Inc., 2000

5. Cash collections from customers for the year were _____.
    a. $450,000
    b. $462,000
    c. $438,000
    d. $365,000

6. Cash payments for inventory during the year was _____.
    a. $207,000
    b. $283,000
    c. $243,000
    d. $233,000

7. Cash paid for supplies during the year was _____.
    a. $9,000
    b. $9,300
    c. $8,700
    d. $10,500

8. Which of the following is a purpose of the cash flow statement?
    a. Assess the entity's ability to generate positive future cash flows.
    b. Assess the entity's ability to meet obligations and pay dividends.
    c. Assess the reasons for differences between income and associated cash receipts and payments.
    d. All of the above are purposes of the cash flow statement.

9. The following selected information is available for the year:

Net income	$400,000
Depreciation expense	67,000
Gain on sale of equipment	9,000
Interest expense	12,000
Increase in accounts receivable	20,000
Increase in accounts payable	1,000
Decrease in interest payable	3,000

What is the company's net cash flow from operations?
    a. $436,000
    b. $400,000
    c. $367,000
    d. $496,000

10. During the year Z Corporation reported interest expense of $65,000 from a bank loan on its income statement. Interest payable had a beginning balance of $2,000 and an ending balance of $7,000. Cash paid for interest during the year was _____.

   a. $65,000
   b. $72,000
   c. $60,000
   d. $70,000

Problem III

Following is a list of important ideas and key concepts from the chapter. To test your knowledge of these terms, match the term with the definition by placing the number in the space provided.

_____ current operating liabilities
_____ direct format
_____ indirect format
_____ noncash current operating asset

1. The format of the statement of cash flows that shows the differences between accrual-based net income and cash flows from operations.

2. A noncash account that represents operating activities.

3. The format of the statement of cash flows that shows the actual cash inflows and outflows of operating activities.

4. Accounts representing operating obligations.

Problem IV

The financial statements of Jax Corporation are present below:

Jax Corporation
Balance Sheet
As of December 31, 19X7 and 19X8

	19X8		19X7	
Current Assets				
Cash	$ 37,000		$ 3,000	
Accounts receivable	85,000		25,000	
Marketable equity securities	9,000		16,000	
Total current assets	$131,000		$ 44,000	
Property, plant and equipment				
Buildings, furniture and equipment $245,000			$260,000	
Less: Accumulated depreciation 85,000	160,000		55,000	205,000
Goodwill		235,000		240,000
Total Assets		$526,000		$489,000
Current Liabilities				
Accounts payable	$ 55,000		$105,000	
Interest payable	13,000		11,000	
Total current liabilities	$ 68,000		$116,000	
Noncurrent Liabilities:				
Mortgage payable		200,000		160,000
Stockholders' Equity:				
Common stock	145,000		130,000	
Paid-in-capital common stock	23,000		18,000	
Retained earnings	90,000		65,000	
		258,000		213,000
Total Liabilities and Stockholders' Equity		$526,000		$489,000

Problem IV (continued)

Jax Corporation
Income Statement
For the Year Ended December 31, 19X8

Revenues:
    Service revenue $650,000
    Gain on sale of equipment   7,000 $657,000

Expenses:
    Selling, general and administrative expenses   540,000
    Depreciation expense   40,000
    Loss on sale of marketable securities   2,000
    Interest expense   10,000
    Goodwill amortization   5,000   597,000
Net Income $ 60,000

Additional information:
1. Jax paid a $35,000 cash dividend to shareholders.
2. Equipment originally costing $15,000 (accumulated depreciation of $10,000) was sold for $12,000.
3. Marketable equity securities originally costing $7,000 were sold for $5,000.

Required: Prepare a statement of cash flows using the indirect method.

Problem V

Use the following legend to indicate in which section of the cash flow statement each accounting event would be reported:

    O   Operating Activities   I   Investing Activities
    F   Financing Activities   NC Noncash Activities

_____ 1. Payment of a cash dividend to stockholders.
_____ 2. Sale of inventory to a customer.
_____ 3. Purchase of equipment to be used in production.
_____ 4. Borrowing money from a local bank.
_____ 5. Purchase of operating supplies.
_____ 6. Payment of salespersons' salaries.
_____ 7. Receipt of interest income from an investment in U.S. Treasury Bills.
_____ 8. Repayment of a short-term note payable.
_____ 9. Issuance of 1,000 shares of common stock.
_____ 10. Purchase of land by issuing a 20-year note payable.
_____ 11. Purchase of a two-year casualty insurance policy.
_____ 12. Purchase of thirty percent of the outstanding stock of X Corporation.

Pause and Reflect

The operating activities section of the statement of cash flows may be presented in either the direct or indirect formats. The FASB suggests that companies use the direct method for presenting cash flows from operations. However, in 1994, *Accounting Trends & Techniques* reported that 97.5 percent of companies used the indirect method to report cash flows from operations. Why would this be the case?

_____
_____
_____
_____
_____
_____
_____
_____
_____

Study Guide, Introduction to Accounting: An Integrated Approach

Solutions for Chapter 25

Problem I

1. T
2. F
3. F
4. F
5. T
6. T
7. T
8. F
9. F
10. T

Problem II

1. b
2. c
3. c
4. d
5. b
6. b
7. b
8. d
9. a
10. c

Problem III

4   current operating liabilities
3   direct format
1   indirect format
2   noncash current operating asset

Problem IV

Jax Corporation
Statement of Cash Flows
For the Year Ended December 31, 19X8

Net Cash Flows from Operating Activities	
Net income	$60,000
Adjustments to Reconcile Net Income to the	
Net Cash Flows from Operations:	
Depreciation expense	40,000
Gain on sale of equipment	< 7,000>
Loss on sale of marketable securities	2,000
Amortization of goodwill	5,000
Deduct increase in accounts receivable	<60,000>
Deduct decrease in accounts payable	<50,000>
Add increase in interest payable	2,000
Cash used by operations	<$8,000>
Net Cash Flows from Investing Activities:	
Sale of equipment	$12,000
Sale of marketable equity securities	5,000
Cash provided by investing activities	$17,000
Net Cash Flows from Financing Activities:	
Borrowing through mortgage payable	40,000
Payment of cash dividends	<35,000>
Issuance of stock	20,000
Cash provided by financing activities	$25,000
Net Change in Cash during 19X8	$34,000
Add: Beginning Balance in Cash	3,000
Ending Balance in Cash	$37,000

Problem V

1. F
2. O
3. I
4. F
5. O
6. O
7. O
8. F
9. F
10. NC
11. O
12. I

Pause and Reflect

The direct method format clearly shows the amounts of cash received and paid for operating activities. However, the direct format involves a large number of adjustments to convert accrual-based revenues and expenses to cash inflows and outflows. In addition, although the FASB suggests that companies use the direct format, the FASB requires companies to disclose a reconciliation of accrual-based net income to the amount of cash flows from operations. This reconciliation is essentially the indirect format of reporting operating cash flows. Therefore, it is cost beneficial in terms of time, effort, and cost to prepare the operating cash flows in the indirect format.

Chapter 26
Firm Performance: A Comprehensive Evaluation

Chapter Overview

Chapter 26 concludes the evaluation phase by examining how external users perform comprehensive financial analysis. The chapter explores the role of capital and information markets and external sources of financial statement comparison information. In addition, the chapter discusses and illustrates how ratios can be used to evaluate the activities of a company. The chapter concludes with a discussion of issues related to the stock market.

As you study this chapter, it will become quickly apparent that you need a thorough understanding of the financial statements and financial statement classifications to perform in-depth financial analysis. You should learn how to calculate the various ratios, but more importantly you should learn to interpret the results of the ratio analysis. You will discover that analysis requires you to look at results over time and to compare results with industry standards. The numbers alone tell you little about a firm's performance.

Read and Recall Questions

> **Learning Objective:**
> L.O.1. Describe the relationships among product and service markets, capital markets, and information markets.

What is the capital market?

How do the investment perspectives of lenders and investors differ?

Describe a free market economy.

Describe the relationship between the product market and the capital market.

Why is there a need for a financial information market?

What are the two problems associated with the market for financial information?

What is the role of the independent auditor in the financial information market?

Learning Objective:
L.O.2. Use financial statement analysis to assess a company's profitability and its short-term and long-term risk.

What are the three primary methods of financial analysis?

What are the benefits of studying comparative financial statements?

Why are external standards necessary for performing financial statement analysis?

Identify at least four sources of external standards.

What is vertical analysis? Is it necessary to compare the results of vertical analysis with external standards? Explain.

What is the purpose of ratio analysis? What types of relationships may be compared with ratios?

What is the purpose of activity ratios?

What is the purpose of the accounts receivable turnover ratio? How is it calculated?

What is the purpose of the inventory turnover ratio? The payables turnover ratio? How are they computed?

Why is it important to assess short-term liquidity and solvency?

What is the purpose of the current ratio? The quick ratio? How are these ratios calculated?

What is cash-flow per share?

What ratios are used by creditors to evaluate a firm's creditworthiness?

What is the purpose of the times interest earned ratio? How is it calculated?

What is the debt-to-equity ratio? How does it differ from the long-term debt to equity ratio?

What is profitability? Why is it important?

What is the purpose of the gross margin ratio? How is it computed?

What is the purpose of the return on assets ratio? The return on owners' equity ratio? Return on common equity? How are these ratios computed?

What is asset turnover? How is the asset turnover ratio calculated?

What is the purpose of the DuPont method of return on investment? How is it calculated?

How is return on sales calculated?

- How is earnings per share calculated?

What does the dividend payout ratio reveal? How is it computed?

> **Learning Objective:**
> L.O.3. Explain why and how financial information and market information can be used to assess a company's investment potential.

What is the purpose of organized stock markets?

- What factors influence the price of stocks?

What is the purpose of the price-earnings ratio? How is it computed?

What is the purpose of the dividend yield ratio? How is it calculated?

Outline of Key Concepts

I. External investors and creditors need to assess overall performance of a company.
   A. Investment decisions are based on the perception of the risk and potential return for each business.
      1. Financial statements are the principal source of information.
   B. There are significant differences between creditors and investors.
      1. Creditors lend a fixed amount of money over a limited term and generally have legal documents that give them legal recourse in recovering their investment from the businesses to which they lend.
      2. Investors have no limited or fixed terms. They commit funds until the business ceases to operate or until they sell their stock to another investor.
         a. They have few guarantees for the money they invest.

II. The relationship among product markets, capital markets, and the information markets.
   A. In the product market, consumers determine the types of goods and services they need and want. Consumer demand creates opportunities for producers to provide these items to consumers.
   B. The capital market is the link between those who produce goods and services and the creditors and investors who own the capital.
      1. The owners of capital want the highest possible return possible, at an appropriate level of risk.
         a. For creditors, the return is the interest rate charged to the borrower plus the amount of change in the market value of debt not held to maturity.
         b. For investors, return consists of the dividends received plus the increase in the value of the stocks held.
      2. External investors and creditors cannot observe business activities, and they do not have ready access to much information about these activities. This creates a market for information.
         a. Producers provide financial information that conforms to GAAP, such as the annual report.
         b. Industry trade publications and government statistics can reveal broader economic factors.

III. Statement analysis for external users.
   A. Comparative financial statements report two or more years' financial statements side by side in a columnar format.
      1. Studying the comparative financial statements helps the reader to become familiar with the company's reporting practices, the accounts and classifications it uses, and the general range of amounts it reflects.
      2. An evaluation of the changes in reported financial data over time helps determine the general trend of operations and assists in deciding whether the company is better or worse off than in previous periods.
         a. See trends as they develop.
         b. Use caution in projecting historical trends into future.
   B. External standards provide an average and a range of quantitative values for ratios of firms in the same or similar industries.
      1. Provides a comparison among investment alternatives.
      2. *RMA Annual Statement Studies* summarizes financial information by industry using Standard Industry Classification (SIC).
      3. *Moody's Handbook of NASDAQ Stocks* and *Moody's Handbook of Common Stocks* provide one-page summaries of the history and principal products as well as detailed financial tables for many of the companies whose stock is traded in the United States.
   C. Vertical analysis may be used to compare financial statement items relative to a base figure.
      1. May compare one company's performance against industry averages.

IV. Ratio analysis makes it easy to compare relationships (1) for firms over time, (2) of different firms, and (3) with standards such as industry averages.
   A. Activity ratios--financial ratios that help in judging a firm's efficiency in using its current assets and liabilities.
      1. Accounts receivable turnover =

$$\frac{\text{Net credit sales}}{\text{Average net accounts receivable}}$$

      2. Average collection period =

$$\frac{365 \text{ days}}{\text{Accounts receivable turnover ratio}}$$

      3. Inventory turnover ratio =

$$\frac{\text{Cost of goods sold}}{\text{Average inventory}}$$

4. Payables turnover =

$$\frac{\text{Total cash expenses}}{\text{Average current liabilities (except bank loans)}}$$

B. Liquidity refers to the cash position of a company and its ability to generate cash inflows through normal operations. Liquidity analysis is concerned with cash flows and the adequacy of current assets to meet current liabilities.
1. Current ratio =

$$\frac{\text{Current assets}}{\text{Current liabilities}}$$

2. Quick ratio =

$$\frac{\text{Cash + Temporary investments + Accounts receivable}}{\text{Current liabilities}}$$

3. Cash flow per share =

$$\frac{\text{Cash flow from operations - Preferred dividends}}{\text{Weighted average number of shares of common stock}}$$

C. Long-term debt-paying ability is typically evaluated with three ratios.
1. Times interest earned =

$$\frac{\text{Net income before interest and taxes}}{\text{Interest expense}}$$

2. Debt-to-equity =

$$\frac{\text{Total liabilities}}{\text{Total shareholders' equity}}$$

a. Measures the extent a company relies on debt rather than ownership financing.

3. Long-term debt to equity =

$$\frac{\text{Total liabilities - Current liabilities - Pension obligations}}{\text{Total shareholders' equity}}$$

D. Profitability is the return on funds invested by the owners and achieved by the efforts of management. It results from operating, investing, and financing decisions over time.

1. Gross margin ratio =

$$\frac{\text{Gross margin}}{\text{Net sales}}$$

2. Return on assets =

$$\frac{\text{Net income}}{\text{Average total assets}}$$

   a. Measures the effectiveness of management in utilizing the resources at its command.

3. Return on owners' equity =

$$\frac{\text{Net income}}{\text{Average owners' equity}}$$

4. Return on common equity =

$$\frac{\text{Net income - Preferred stock dividends}}{\text{Stockholders' equity - Liquidating value of preferred stock}}$$

5. Asset turnover =

$$\frac{\text{Net sales}}{\text{Average total assets}}$$

   a. Relates a firm's ability to generate sales to the amount of assets that the firm employs.

6. Return on sales =

$$\frac{\text{Net income}}{\text{Net sales}}$$

7. Du Pont ROI =

$$\frac{\text{Net sales}}{\text{Average total assets}} \times \frac{\text{Net income}}{\text{Net sales}}$$

8. Earnings per share =

$$\frac{\text{Net income - Preferred dividends}}{\text{Weighted-average number of shares of common stock}}$$

9. Dividend payout ratio =

$$\frac{\text{Dividends paid to common stockholders}}{\text{Earnings available to common stockholders}}$$

   a. Reveals a firm's dividend payment philosophy.

10. Price-earnings ratio =

$$\frac{\text{Current market price}}{\text{Earnings per share}}$$

   a. Reflects the relationship between the earnings of a firm and the market price of its common stock.
   b. Is an approximation of the market's assessment of a company's prospective earnings performance.

11. Dividend yield =

$$\frac{\text{Dividends paid per share of stock}}{\text{Market price per share of stock}}$$

   a. Measures the cash return as a percentage of the stock's current price.
   b. Does not measure the return from appreciation of the stock price.

V. Stock markets allow numerous transactions involving the purchase and sale of corporate stock on a daily basis.
  A. Stock prices vary on a daily basis.
    1. Prospects for greater profits push stock prices up.
    2. Prospects for lower profits push stock prices down.

Problem I

Indicate whether the following statements are either true (T) or false (F).

_____ 1. In a free market economy, consumer demand determines the nature of businesses that exists and how much of a given product or service is available.
_____ 2. The debt-to-equity ratio measures the extent that a company relies on debt rather than equity to finance operations.
_____ 3. Free market economies rely on government to dictate the type of businesses and the amount of a product or service to provide.
_____ 4. Most potential investments offer the same risk and return.
_____ 5. Financial statements are difficult to interpret without an external standard against which they can be compared.
_____ 6. One means of assessing a business's liquidity is through the use of activity ratios.
_____ 7. The dividend yield does not take into account the return from appreciation in the stock price.
_____ 8. The earnings per share ratio is an approximation of the market's assessment of a company's prospective earnings performance.
_____ 9. In vertical analysis, each balance sheet item is divided by total assets.
_____ 10. The quick ratio provides a more conservative measure of short-term liquidity than the current ratio.

Problem II

Indicate the correct answer by circling the appropriate letter.

1. Which of the following is not considered a liquidity ratio?
    a. Current ratio.
    b. Payables turnover ratio.
    c. Quick ratio.
    d. Cash flow per share ratio.

2. Ratio analysis makes it easy to compare relationships _____.
    a. for a company over time
    b. of different companies
    c. with standards such as industry averages
    d. All of the above are correct.

Use the following information for the next four questions:
Selected information for the Y Corporation is presented below:

    Net sales $100,000
    Net income $ 20,000
    Average total assets $400,000
    Earnings per share $1.2
    Current market price per share $10
    Average stockholders' equity $160,000

3. The price-earnings ratio is _____.
   a. 8.333
   b. 12.1
   c. 6.7
   d. .12

4. Y Corporation has no preferred stock outstanding. During the year, the company paid $2,000 in dividends to common shareholders. The dividend payout ratio is _____.
   a. 5%
   b. 20%
   c. 32%
   d. 10%

5. The return on sales is _____.
   a. 10%
   b. 15%
   c. 20%
   d. 25%

6. The return on total assets is _____.
   a. 5%
   b. 20%
   c. 32%
   d. 1%

7. Which of the following is not considered an activity ratio?
   a. Accounts receivable turnover ratio.
   b. Inventory turnover ratio.
   c. Average collection period ratio.
   d. Current ratio.

8. Z Corporation's accounts receivable turnover ratio was 12.1 for the year. The average collection period would be _____.
   a. 30.16 days
   b. 25.78 days
   c. 12.1 days
   d. 62.7 days

9. Which of the following ratios is not used to assess a firm's profitability?
   a. Return on assets ratio.
   b. Return on owners' equity ratio.
   c. Gross margin ratio.
   d. All of the above are used assess profitability.

10. Z Corporation has 10,000 shares of $5 par value common stock and 1,000 shares of $100 par, 10% cumulative preferred stock outstanding. Net income for the year was $140,000 and total stockholders' equity is $600,000. The liquidation value of the preferred stock is its par value. Return on common equity for the year is _____.
    a. 12%
    b. 18%
    c. 22%
    d. 26%

Problem III

Following is a list of important ideas and key concepts from the chapter. To test your knowledge of these terms, match the term with the definition by placing the number in the space provided.

_____ asset turnover ratio
_____ capital market
_____ cash flow per share
_____ dividend payout ratio
_____ dividend yield ratio

_____ earnings multiple (price-earnings ratio)
_____ free market economy
_____ price-earnings (PE) ratio
_____ return on common equity ratio

1. An economy in which consumer demand determines the nature of businesses that exist and how much of a given product or service is available

2. A ratio that investors use to evaluate potential stock investments based on the relationship between the current market price of the stock relative to the firm's current earnings per share

3. A profitability ratio for common stockholders that adjusts the ratio of net income to stockholders' equity for their respective preferred stock components

4. A ratio that reveals a firm's dividend payment philosophy by relating the amount of dividends paid to common stockholders to the period's earnings available to common stockholders to assess the prospects for future cash flows paid directly to stockholders

5. A measure of a firm's liquidity based on using the amount of cash flow from operations less preferred dividends on a per share basis

6. The entire group of creditors and investors who provide capital to businesses to allow them to finance their investments

7. A stock's price divided by its annual net income (PE ratio), which is a measure used by investors to decide whether to buy, sell, or hold a particular stock

8. A ratio that measures profitability by relating a firm's ability to generate sales (net sales) to the amount of assets (average total assets) that the firm employs

9. A ratio that measures the return an investor would receive on a company's stock at the current price, if recent dividend payments continue into the foreseeable future

Problem IV

Complete the following sentences by filling in the correct response.

1. The group of creditors and investors who provide capital to businesses make up what is referred to as the _____ _____.

2. Investors invest money in companies expecting return in the form of _____ and/or _____ _____ for the stock they hold.

3. Financial statements provide information that is used to assess a company's _____, longer-term debt-paying ability, and _____.

4. _____ ratios are helpful in judging a company's efficiency in using its _____ assets and liabilities.

5. The inventory turnover ratio is calculated by taking _____ and dividing it by average _____.

6. The payables turnover is calculated by taking _____ and dividing by average _____ except for _____.

7. The quick ratio is calculated by taking the _____ plus _____ plus _____ and dividing the amount by the total _____.

8. The _____, _____ and _____ ratios are used to assess a company's long-term debt-paying ability.

9. The debt-to-equity ratio is calculated by dividing _____ by _____.

10. The return on common equity is calculated by dividing _____ less any _____ by _____ minus the _____ value of preferred stock.

11. The Du Pont ROI is calculated by taking the _____ ratio times the _____ ratio.

12. The price-earnings ratio is calculated by taking the current _____ and dividing by the _____.

293

©The McGraw-Hill Companies, Inc., 2000

Problem V

The financial statements of Zectar Corporation are present below:

Zectar Corporation
Balance Sheet
As of December 31, 19X7 and 19X8

	19X8		19X7	
Current Assets				
Cash		$ 37,000		$ 3,000
Accounts receivable		85,000		25,000
Inventory		120,000		90,000
Marketable equity securities		9,000		16,000
Total current assets		$251,000		$134,000
Property, plant and equipment				
Buildings, furniture and equipment	$245,000		$260,000	
Less: Accumulated depreciation	85,000	160,000	55,000	205,000
Other Assets				
Goodwill		235,000		240,000
Total Assets		$646,000		$579,000
Current Liabilities				
Accounts payable		$175,000		$195,000
Interest payable		13,000		11,000
Total current liabilities		$188,000		$206,000
Noncurrent Liabilities:				
Bonds payable		200,000		160,000
Stockholders' Equity:				
Common stock		145,000		130,000
Paid-in-capital common stock		23,000		18,000
Retained earnings		90,000		65,000
		258,000		213,000
Total Liabilities and Stockholders' Equity		$646,000		$579,000

Problem V (continued)

Zectar Corporation
Income Statement
For the Year Ended December 31, 19X8

Revenues:
    Net Sales (all on credit) $700,000

Expenses:
    Cost of goods sold   340,000
    Selling, general and administrative expenses   235,000
    Depreciation expense   40,000
    Interest expense   10,000   625,000

Net Income $ 75,000

Required: Calculate the following ratios for Zectar Corporation for 19X8.

1. Current ratio.

2. Accounts receivable turnover ratio.

3. Inventory turnover ratio.

4. Quick ratio.

5. Debt-to-equity ratio.

©The McGraw-Hill Companies, Inc., 2000

6. Gross margin ratio.

7. Return on owners' equity ratio.

8. Du Pont ROI ratio.

Pause and Reflect

Scott and Sandy have been searching for "good" investment opportunities. While evaluating the financial information available from two companies, Company A and Company B, they began discussing the difference in the companies' dividend yield ratios. Company A's dividend yield was much higher than Company B's yield. Sandy said that she knew that some companies pay out a large portion of their earnings in dividends while other companies paid few or no dividends. She also told Scott that dividends affect the value of stock and that it is better to invest in stocks that have high dividend yields. Scott agrees that companies may have dividend payment policies, but he doesn't agree that you should always invest in the company with the highest dividend yield. Who is correct and why?

Solutions for Chapter 26

Problem I

1. T
2. T
3. F
4. F
5. T
6. F
7. T
8. F
9. T
10. T

Problem II

1. b
2. d
3. a
4. d
5. c
6. a
7. d
8. a
9. d
10. d

Problem III

8	asset turnover ratio	7	earnings multiple (price-earnings ratio)
6	capital market	1	free market economy
5	cash flow per share	2	price-earnings (PE) ratio
4	dividend payout ratio	3	return on common equity ratio
9	dividend yield ratio		

Problem IV

1. capital market
2. dividends, higher prices
3. liquidity, profitability
4. Activity, current
5. cost of goods sold, inventory
6. total cash expenses, current liabilities, bank loans
7. cash, temporary investments, accounts receivable, current liabilities
8. times interest earned, debt-to-equity, long-term debt-to-equity
9. total liabilities, total shareholders' equity
10. net income, preferred stock dividends, stockholders' equity, liquidating
11. asset turnover, return on sales
12. market price, earnings per share

Problem V

1. Current ratio $= \dfrac{\$251,000}{\$188,000} = 1.34$

2. Accounts receivable turnover $= \dfrac{\$700,000}{(\$85,000 + \$25,000)/2} = 12.73$

3. Inventory turnover $= \dfrac{\$340,000}{(\$120,000 + \$90,000)/2} = 3.24$

4. Quick ratio $= \dfrac{\$37,000 + \$85,000 + \$9,000}{\$188,000} = .697$

5. Debt-to-equity ratio $= \dfrac{\$388,000}{\$258,000} = 1.5$

6. Gross margin ratio $= \dfrac{\$700,000 - \$340,000}{\$700,000} = 51.4\%$

7. Return on owners' equity ratio = $\dfrac{\$75,000}{(\$258,000 + \$213,000)/2}$ = 31.9%

8. Du Pont ROI ratio = $\dfrac{\$700,000}{(\$646,000 + \$579,000)/2} \times \dfrac{\$75,000}{\$700,000}$ = 12.3%

Pause and Reflect

Scott is correct. The amount of dividends that a company pays depends partially on its investment opportunities. Companies with good opportunities will usually pay lower dividends. Their cash is used to acquire additional assets for the company. Often these companies are in high-growth industries. More mature, stable companies with fewer investment opportunities will often pay large dividends. Low-dividend-payout companies are often high-value companies that are relatively risky compared to high-payout companies. An investor must decide on the amount of risk he or she is willing to accept and whether he or she is investing for growth and higher future income or for current cash flows.